Funded by the EU-China Managers Exchange and Training Programme
中国—欧盟经理人交流培训项目资助

Winning in China

—Business Chinese

赢在中国

基础篇3
Basic 3

——商务汉语系列教程

- 编委会主任　王正富

- 编委会委员　曹红月　王福明　韩维春　季　瑾　李英海

- 主编　季　瑾

- 编者　季　瑾　崔艳蕾　杨康丽　潘景景　窦小力

北京语言大学出版社
BEIJING LANGUAGE AND CULTURE
UNIVERSITY PRESS

图书在版编目（CIP）数据

赢在中国：商务汉语系列教程. 基础篇. 3 / 季瑾
主编. —北京：北京语言大学出版社，2010. 8（2015. 2 重印）
ISBN 978-7-5619-2843-1

Ⅰ.①赢…　Ⅱ.①季…　Ⅲ.①商务－汉语－对外汉语
教学－教材　Ⅳ.①H195. 4

中国版本图书馆 CIP 数据核字（2010）第 167642 号

封面图片来源：gettyimages

书　　名：赢在中国——商务汉语系列教程·基础篇3
英文翻译：赵瑞华
责任印制：汪学发

出版发行：北京语言大学出版社
社　　址：北京市海淀区学院路 15 号　　邮政编码：100083
网　　址：www. blcup. com
电　　话：发行部　82303650/3591/3651
　　　　　编辑部　82303647
　　　　　读者服务部　82303653
　　　　　网上订购电话　82303908
　　　　　客户服务信箱　service@ blcup. com
印　　刷：北京联兴盛业印刷股份有限公司
经　　销：全国新华书店

版　　次：2010 年 8 月第 1 版　2015 年 2 月第 2 次印刷
开　　本：889 毫米×1194 毫米　1/16　印张：11. 5
字　　数：241 千字
书　　号：ISBN 978-7-5619-2843-1/H·10220
定　　价：38. 00 元

凡有印装质量问题，本社负责调换。电话：82303590

目 录
CONTENTS

词类简称表 Abbreviations of parts of speech ·· I

语法术语简称表 Abbreviations of grammatical terms ·· II

主要人物介绍 Introduction of the main characters ·· III

第十一单元 UNIT 11　你哪儿不舒服 What's wrong with you　看病 Seeing a doctor

课文一 Text 1：挂号费多少钱　　　　　　　　　　　　　　2

How much is the registration fee

注释 Notes：

1．"大夫"

2．结构助词"得"及程度补语

The structural particle "得" and the complement of degree

课文二 Text 2：先给你开点儿药吧　　　　　　　　　　　　6

I'll prescribe some medicine for you

注释 Notes：

1．动词"算"　The verb "算"

2．"把"字句　The "把" sentence

3．名词"刚才"　The noun "刚才"

辨析："刚才"、"刚"　Discrimination："刚才" and "刚"

4．副词"差不多"（复习）　The adverb "差不多" (Review)

课文三 Text 3：你哪儿不舒服　What's wrong with you　　　13

注释 Notes：

1．不带"得"的程度补语　The complement of degree without "得"

2．由数量短语构成的名词谓语句

A noun-predicate sentence composed of numeral-classifier compounds

3．动词"注意"　The verb "注意"

赢在中国
——商务汉语系列教程 基础篇 3

课文四 Text 4：祝他早日康复   17
I hope he will get well soon

注释 Notes：

1. 疑问代词"怎么样" The interrogative pronoun "怎么样"
   辨析："怎么样"、"怎么" Discrimination: "怎么样" and "怎么"
2. "被"字句 The "被" sentence
3. 副词"只是" The adverb "只是"
4. 连动句 The serial-verb sentence
5. 动词"祝" The verb "祝"

练习 Exercises   25

第十二单元 Unit 12 你打算租什么样的房子
What kind of apartment do you want to rent
租房
Renting an apartment

课文一 Text 1：你打算租什么样的房子   37
What kind of apartment do you want to rent

注释 Notes：

1. 叹词"嘿" The interjection "嘿"
2. 副词"一直" The adverb "一直"
3. 副词"最好" The adverb "最好"
4. 表示假设关系的复句："如果……，就……"（复习）
   The compound sentence denoting a suppositional relation: "如果……，就……" (Review)
5. 指示代词"有的" The demonstrative pronoun "有的"
6. 单音节形容词的重叠 The reduplicate form of a monosyllabic adjective
7. 兼语句 The pivotal sentence
8. 表示让步关系的复句："A 倒是 A，可是 B"
   The compound sentence denoting concession: "A倒是A，可是B"
9. "想起来了"
10. 动词"拜托" The verb "拜托"

课文二 Text 2：一平米一天多少钱呢   48
What's the rent for one square meter per day

注释 Notes：

1. "我想问一下"

2. "多 + 长 / 大 / 重 / 高"

3. 主谓谓语句（复习） The subject-predicate predicate sentence (Review)

4. 用 "有没有" 的正反疑问句

   The affirmative-negative question with "有没有"

5. 动词 "过来"（复习） The verb "过来"（Review）

课文三 Text 3：康爱丽的办公室 Alice's office   54

注释 Notes：

1. 转折复句："虽然……，但是……"

   The transitional compound sentence "虽然……，但是……"

2. 动态助词 "着" 及存在句

   The aspect particle "着" and the existential sentence

练习 Exercises   59

第十三单元
Unit 13

我要开一个储蓄账户
I want to open a savings account

在银行
At the bank

课文一 Text 1：您要办什么业务 Can I help you   70
注释 Notes：

1. "（是）……，还是……"

2. "比" 字句（复习） The "比" sentence (Review)

3. 无主语兼语句 The pivotal sentence without a subject

4. 副词 "经常" The adverb "经常"

5. 多项状语的顺序 The sequence of multiple adverbial modifiers

6. 副词 "顺便" The adverb "顺便"

课文二 Text 2：我来银行取点儿钱　　　　　　　　　78
I come to the bank to withdraw some money

注释 **Notes**：

1．"没想到"

2．形容词"巧"　The adjective "巧"

3．"不 A 也不 B"

4．动词"爆"　The verb "爆"

5．叹词"哦"　The interjection "哦"

6．副词"原来"　The adverb "原来"

7．"原来是这样"

8．指示代词"这么"　The demonstrative pronoun "这么"

9．副词"好像"　The adverb "好像"

课文三 Text 3：分期付款　Payment by installment　　　84
注释 **Notes**：

1．"很"＋"有"/ 表示心理感知的动词

"很"＋"有"/ The verb denoting mental perception

2．程度副词"比较"　The degree adverb "比较"

练习 Exercises　　　　　　　　　　　　　　　　　87

第十四单元 Unit 14　**你可以网上购物**
You can shop online

网上购物 Shopping online

课文一 Text 1：你可以网上购物　You can shop online　　　96
注释 **Notes**：

1．表示假设关系的复句："要是……，就……"
The compound sentence with "要是……，就……" denoting a suppositional relation

2．动词＋"着"（＋"也"）＋形容词　The structure "V＋着（＋也）＋Adj"

3．语气助词"呀"　The modal particle "呀"

4．副词"几乎"　The adverb "几乎"

5．副词"才"　The adverb "才"

6. 用"是不是"的正反疑问句
The affirmative-negative question with "是不是"

7. 语气助词"啊"　The modal particle "啊"

课文二 Text 2：是 B2B 电子商务网上贸易平台吗　104
Is it the online trading platform for B2B
electronic commerce

注释 Notes：

1. B2B（Business to Business）

2. 指示代词"这样"　The demonstrative pronoun "这样"

课文三 Text 3：电子商务又省时又省力　108
Electronic business saves a lot of time and
energy

注释 Notes：

1. "从……来看"

2. 习惯用语"可不是"　The idiom "可不是"

3. 叹词"嗬"　The interjection "嗬"

4. 介词"连"　The preposition "连"

5. 语气助词"嘛"（复习）　The modal particle "嘛"（Review）

练习 Exercices　115

第十五单元　希望您在这儿过得愉快　在宾馆
Unit 15　Wish you a good time here　At the hotel

课文一 Text 1：我想预订房间　124
I'll like to reserve a room

注释 Notes：

1. 征询语及礼貌用语　The inquiring expressions and polite expressions

2. 动词"需要"　The verb "需要"

3. 动词"帮助"　The verb "帮助"

4. 副词"大约"　The adverb "大约"

5. 动词"差" The verb "差"

6. 敬辞"贵" The term of respect "贵"

7. 介词"按" The preposition "按"

8. 形容词"紧张" The adjective "紧张"

课文二 Text 2：你打算怎么安排　　　　　　**132**
What arrangement will you make for him

注释 Notes：

1. 副词"将" The adverb "将"

2. 动词"希望" The verb "希望"

3. 连词"此外" The conjunction "此外"

4. 副词"极" The adverb "极"

5. 介词"为" The preposition "为"

6. 介词"由" The preposition "由"

课文三 Text 3：您有什么需要尽管说　　　　　　**139**
Please don't hesitate to tell me whenever you need help

注释 Notes：

1. 副词"尽管" The adverb "尽管"

2. "有朋自远方来，不亦乐乎！"

3. 结构助词"地" The structural particle "地"

练习 Exercises　　　　　　**146**

生词总表 Vocabulary　　　　　　**153**

词类简称表
Abbreviations of parts of speech

缩写 Abbreviations	英文全称 Parts of speech in English	词类名称 Parts of speech in Chinese	拼音 Parts of speech in *pinyin*
Adj	Adjective	形容词	xíngróngcí
Adv	Adverb	副词	fùcí
AP	Aspect Particle	动态助词	dòngtài zhùcí
Conj	Conjunction	连词	liáncí
IE	Idiom Expression	习惯用语	xíguàn yòngyǔ
Int	Interjection	叹词	tàncí
LN	Locality Noun	方位词	fāngwèicí
M	Measure Word	量词	liàngcí
MdPt	Modal Particle	语气助词	yǔqì zhùcí
N	Noun	名词	míngcí
Nu	Numeral	数词	shùcí
Ono	Onomatopoeia	象声词	xiàngshēngcí
OpV.	Optative Verb	能愿动词	néngyuàn dòngcí
PN	Proper Noun	专有名词	zhuānyǒu míngcí
Pr	Pronoun	代词	dàicí
Pref	Prefix	词头	cítóu
Prep	Preposition	介词	jiècí
Pt	Particle	助词	zhùcí
PW	Place Word	地点词	dìdiǎncí
Q	Quantifier	数量词	shùliàngcí
QPr	Question Pronoun	疑问代词	yíwèn dàicí
QPt	Question Particle	疑问助词	yíwèn zhùcí
StPt	Structural Particle	结构助词	jiégòu zhùcí
Suf	Suffix	词尾	cíwěi
TW	Time Word	时间词	shíjiāncí
V	Verb	动词	dòngcí
V//O	Verb-object Compound	离合词	líhécí

语法术语简称表
Abbreviations of grammatical terms

缩写 Abbreviations	英文全称 Grammatical terms in English	语法术语 Grammatical terms in Chinese	拼音 Grammatical terms in *pinyin*
S	Subject	主语	zhǔyǔ
P	Predicate	谓语	wèiyǔ
O	Object	宾语	bīnyǔ
Attr	Attribute	定语	dìngyǔ
A	Adverbial	状语	zhuàngyǔ
Comp	Complement	补语	bǔyǔ
NP	Noun Phrase	名词短语	míngcí duǎnyǔ
VP	Verbal Phrase	动词短语	dòngcí duǎnyǔ
PP	Prepositional Phrase	介词短语	jiècí duǎnyǔ
V O	Verb-object Phrase	动宾短语	dòng-bīn duǎnyǔ
	Declarative Sentence	陈述句	chénshùjù
	Interrogative Sentence	疑问句	yíwènjù
	Affirmative Sentence	肯定句	kěndìngjù
	Negative Sentence	否定句	fǒudìngjù
	General Interrogative Sentence	一般疑问句	yìbān yíwènjù
	Special Interrogative Sentence	特殊疑问句	tèshū yíwènjù
	Yes-or-no Question	是非疑问句	shìfēi yíwènjù
	Affirmative and Negative Question	正反疑问句	zhèngfǎn yíwènjù

主要人物介绍
Introduction of the main characters

Kǎ'ěr
卡尔
Karl Hofmann

Kāng Àilì
康爱丽
Alice Clement

Lǐ Míngming
李明明
Li Mingming

Zhāng Yuǎn
张远
Zhang Yuan

卡　尔——男，德国人，欧盟经理人；
康爱丽——女，法国人，欧盟经理人；
李明明——女，中国人，对外经济贸易大学国贸专业本科三年级学生；
张　远——男，中国人，对外经济贸易大学MBA二年级学生。

　　康爱丽、卡尔都是来北京接受汉语培训的欧盟经理人，李明明和张远是他们在对外经济贸易大学认识的朋友。

Ka'er—Karl Hofmann, male, a German manager from the European Union;

Kang Aili—Alice Clement, female, a French manager from the European Union;

Li Mingming—female, a Chinese junior majoring in International Trade at University of International Business and Economics;

Zhang Yuan—male, a Chinese MBA sophomore at University of International Business and Economics.

　　Both Kang Aili (Alice) and Ka'er (Karl) are managers from the European Union who came to Beijing for the training of Chinese language. Li Mingming and Zhang Yuan are their friends at University of International Business and Economics.

课文 Text	题目 Title	注释 Notes
一	挂号费多少钱 How much is the registration fee	1. "大夫" 2. 结构助词"得"及程度补语 The structural particle "得" and the complement of degree
二	先给你开点儿药吧 I'll prescribe some medicine for you	1. 动词"算" The verb "算" 2. "把"字句 The "把" sentence 3. 名词"刚才" The noun "刚才" 辨析："刚才"、"刚" Discrimination："刚才" and "刚" 4. 副词"差不多"（复习） The adverb "差不多" (Review)
三	你哪儿不舒服 What's wrong with you	1. 不带"得"的程度补语 The complement of degree without "得" 2. 由数量短语构成的名词谓语句 A noun-predicate sentence composed of numeral-classifier compounds 3. 动词"注意" The verb "注意"
四	祝他早日康复 I hope he will get well soon	1. 疑问代词"怎么样" The interrogative pronoun "怎么样" 辨析："怎么样"、"怎么" Discrimination: "怎么样" and "怎么" 2. "被"字句 The "被" sentence 3. 副词"只是" The adverb "只是" 4. 连动句 The serial-verb sentence 5. 动词"祝" The verb "祝"

Guàhàofèi Duōshao Qián

挂号费多少钱

How much is the registration fee

Kāng Àilì bìng le, tā láidào yīyuàn.

康爱丽病了，她来到医院。

Alice is sick and she is now at the information desk of the out-patient department of the hospital.

Kāng Àilì: Dàifu, wǒ tóu téng, guà shénme kē?

● 康爱丽： 大夫，我头疼，挂什么科？

Alice: Doctor, I have a headache. Which department should I register for?

Hùshi: Nǐ kěyǐ zài ménzhěnbù guà nèikē. Yǒu bìnglìběn ma?

○ 护士： 你可以在门诊部挂内科。有病历本吗？

Nurse: You can register for the Internal Medicine Department at out-patient department. Do you have the case history book?

Kāng Àilì: Méiyǒu. Guàhàofèi duōshao qián?

● 康爱丽： 没有。挂号费多少钱？

Alice: No. How much is the registration fee?

Hùshi: Zhuānjiāhào shísì, pǔtōnghào wǔ kuài. Guàhào de shíhou yào mǎi ge
○ 护士：   专家号 14，普通号 5 块。挂号的时候要买个

               bìnglìběn.
               病历本。

Nurse: 14 *kuai* for registration for a specialist and 5 *kuai* for a common registration.

             And you need to buy a case history book when you register.

Kāng Àilì: Wǒ téng de lìhai, néng mǎshàng kàn ma?
● 康爱丽：   我疼得厉害，能马上看吗？

Alice: My head is aching terribly. Can I see the doctor right away?

Hùshi: Nà nǐ qù kàn jízhěn ba.
○ 护士：   那你去看急诊吧。

Nurse: Then please go to the Emergency Department.

Kāng Àilì: Zěnme zǒu?
● 康爱丽：   怎么走？

Alice: How can I get there?

Hùshi: Zhí zǒu, yòu zhuǎn jiù dào le.
○ 护士：   直走，右转就到了。

Nurse: Go straight and turn right, and then you will find it.

生词 Shēngcí **New Words**

1. 挂号	guà hào	V//O	to register (at a hospital, etc.)
2. 费	fèi	N	expense, fee
3. 大夫	dàifu	N	doctor
4. 头	tóu	N	head
5. 疼	téng	Adj	ache
6. 挂	guà	V	to register
7. 科	kē	N	department
8. 护士	hùshi	N	nurse
9. 门诊部	ménzhěnbù	N	out-patient department

10.	内科	nèikē	N	internal medicine
11.	病历	bìnglì	N	medical record, case history
12.	本	běn	N	notebook
13.	专家	zhuānjiā	N	expert, specialist
14.	号	hào	N	registration
15.	普通	pǔtōng	Adj	common
16.	厉害	lìhai	Adj	terrible
17.	马上	mǎshàng	Adv	at once, soon
18.	看	kàn	V	to see (a doctor)
19.	急诊	jízhěn	N	emergency treatment
20.	直	zhí	Adv	directly, straight
21.	转	zhuǎn	V	to turn, to shift, to change

注释 Zhùshì **Notes**

1 **大夫，我头疼。Doctor, I have a headache.**

"大夫"，这里是康爱丽对护士的称呼，是客气的说法。中国人在医院时往往把医生、护士等工作人员都统称为"大夫"。

Alice addresses the nurse as "大夫" in a polite way. Chinese people usually address doctors, nurses and other staff in the hospital as "大夫".

2 **我疼得厉害。My head is aching terribly.**

"得（de）"，结构助词，用在形容词或表示感觉、感情、心理活动的动词后面，连接表示程度的补语。基本结构：主语＋形容词／动词＋"得"＋程度补语。能作程度补语的词语有："很、多、要死（yàosǐ, extremely, awfally, terribly）、要命（yào mìng, extremely, terribly）、不得了（bù déliǎo, extremely, exceedingly）、不行、厉害"等，一般都表示程度高。例如：

"得", a structural particle, is put after the adjective or the verb which denotes mental perception to connect with the complement of degree. The basic structure is "subject + adjective / verb + 得 +

complement of degree". The following words can serve as the complement of degree: "很", "多", "要死", "要命", "不得了", "不行", and "厉害", etc. They usually indicate a high degree. For example,

S	Adj / V	StPt（得）	Degree Comp
我的书	多		很。
他	忙	得	要死。
我们	累		不行。

Xiān Gěi Nǐ Kāi Diǎnr Yào ba

先给你开点儿药吧

I'll prescribe some medicine for you

Kāng Àilì zài jízhěnshì li.

康爱丽在急诊室里。

Alice is in the emergency room.

Kāng Àilì: Dàifu, wǒ tóu téng de hěn.

● 康爱丽: 大夫，我头疼得很。

Alice: Doctor, I have a bad headache.

Yīshēng: Fāshāo ma?

○ 医生: 发烧吗？

Doctor: Do you have a fever?

Kāng Àilì: Tóu yǒudiǎnr rè.

● 康爱丽: 头有点儿热。

Alice: A little bit in the head.

Yīshēng: Xiān qù liáng yíxià tǐwēn.

○ 医生: 先去量一下体温。

Doctor: Take a temperature first.

Kāng Àilì liángwán le, yīshēng kànle kàn tǐwēnjì.

康爱丽量完了，医生看了看体温计。

After Alice took the temperature, the doctor had a look at the thermometer.

Yīshēng: Sānshíbā dù, bú suàn gāo. Sǎngzi téng ma?

● 医生： 38℃，不算高。嗓子疼吗？

Doctor: 38℃. Not too high. Does the throat hurt?

Kāng Àilì: Yǒudiǎnr téng.

○ 康爱丽： 有点儿疼。

Alice: A little bit.

Yīshēng: Bǎ zuǐ zhāngkāi, wǒ kànkan.

● 医生： 把嘴张开，我看看。

Doctor: Open your mouth and let me have a look.

Kāng Àilì zhāngkāi zuǐ, yīshēng kànle kàn.

康爱丽张开嘴，医生看了看。

Alice opens the mouth and the doctor has a look.

Yīshēng: Sǎngzi yǒudiǎnr fāyán. Nǐ késou、liú bítì ma?

● 医生： 嗓子有点儿发炎。你咳嗽、流鼻涕吗？

Doctor: Your throat has a little bit inflammation. Do you cough or have a running nose?

Kāng Àilì: Bù késou, bù liú bítì. Duì le, gāngcái dǎle jǐ ge pēntì.

○ 康爱丽： 不咳嗽，不流鼻涕。对了，刚才打了几个喷嚏。

Alice: No, I don't cough. Nor do I have a running nose. Oh, I sneezed just now.

Yīshēng: Nǐ gǎnmào le, búguò bú lìhai. Xiān gěi nǐ kāi diǎnr yào ba.

● 医生： 你感冒了，不过不厉害。先给你开点儿药吧。

Doctor: You've got a cold, but not a serious one. I'll prescribe some medicine for you.

Kāng Àilì: Dàifu, wǒ hòutiān yào chūchāi, bìng néng hǎo ma?

○ 康爱丽： 大夫，我后天要出差，病能好吗？

Alice: Doctor, I will go on a business trip the day after tomorrow. Can I get recovered by then?

Yīshēng: Nà jiù shūyè ba, shūyè hǎo de kuài.

● 医生： 那就输液吧，输液好得快。

Doctor: Then you'd better get an infusion. It helps you get recovered faster.

Kāng Àilì: Nà děi shū duō cháng shíjiān?

○ 康爱丽： 那得输多长时间？

Alice: How long does it take?

Yīshēng: Bù cháng, chàbuduō sìshí fēnzhōng ba.

● 医生： 不长，差不多40分钟吧。

Doctor: Not long. About 40 minutes.

Kāng Àilì: Xièxie dàifu!

○ 康爱丽： 谢谢大夫！

Alice: Thank you, doctor.

生词 Shēngcí New Words

1.	开	kāi	V	to prescribe
2.	药	yào	N	medicine
3.	发烧	fā shāo	V//O	to have a fever
4.	量	liáng	V	to take (one's temperature), to measure
5.	体温	tǐwēn	N	body temperature
6.	算	suàn	V	to count as, to treat as
7.	嗓子	sǎngzi	N	throat
8.	把	bǎ	Prep	*used to bring out the patient of a verb*
9.	嘴	zuǐ	N	mouth
10.	张	zhāng	V	to open
11.	发炎	fāyán	V	to inflame
12.	咳嗽	késou	V	to cough

13. 流	liú	V	to flow
14. 鼻涕	bítì	N	snot
15. 刚才	gāngcái	N	just now
16. 喷嚏	pēntì	N	sneeze
17. 感冒	gǎnmào	V	to have a cold
18. 出差	chū chāi	V//O	to go on a business trip
19. 病	bìng	N/V	illness; to be ill
20. 输液	shū yè	V//O	to transfuse, to infuse

注释 Zhùshì **Notes**

1 **38℃，不算高。 38℃. Not too high.**

"算"，动词，这里是"当做、可以说"的意思。可以带动词、形容词、名词、数量词、小句作宾语。这时，"算"不能带"了、过"，不能重叠。例如：

"算", a verb, has the same meaning as "当做" or "可以说". It can be followed by a verb, an adjective, a noun, a quantifier, or a clause as the objective, but it cannot be followed by "了" or "过". In addition, it cannot be reduplicated. For example,

① 今年夏天不算热。

② 这些苹果就算 10 块钱吧。

③ 这件事儿算你说对了。

④ 这次还算不上失败（shībài, to fail）。

2 **把嘴张开。 Open your mouth.**

"把"字句，表示对人或事物的处置。主语是动作的发出者，是施事，介词"把"引出受事。谓语动词所表示的动作对受事施加影响，使它发生某种变化或产生某种结果。基本结构：主语＋"把"＋宾语＋谓语动词＋其他成分。例如：

The "把" sentence indicates to handle or deal with somebody or something. The subject is the initiator of the action or the agent. The preposition "把" brings out the patient. The action denoted by the predicate exerts influence on the patient and makes it change or cause some effect. The basic structure is "subject + 把 + object + predicate verb + other elements". For example,

S	A	Prep（把）	O	V	Other elements
他	没		水	喝	完。
你	可以		书包	放	在桌子上。
李明明		把	衣服	洗	了。
卡尔	不应该		"大"	写	成"太"。
你	别		书	给	他。
（1）	（2）	（3）	（4）	（5）（6）	（7）（8）

（1）主语是谓语动词所表示的动作的发出者。例如：

The subject is the initiator of the action denoted by the predicate verb. For example,

① 我把水喝完了。（"水"是"我""喝"的 The "water" is "drunk" by "me". ）

② 她把书放在桌子上。（"书"是"她""放"的 The "book" is "placed" by "her". ）

（2）能愿动词、否定副词等一般放在"把"的前面，不能放在"把"的后面。

The modal verbs and negative adverbs are usually put before "把", not after it.

（3）介词"把"和它后面的宾语构成介词短语作状语。

The preposition "把", together with the object after it, forms a prepositional phrase serving as the adverbial modifier.

（4）"把"字句的宾语必须是定指的或是听话人知道的，如"这辆车、那张报纸、小王的电脑"。在大多数的"把"字句中，"把"的宾语和全句的谓语动词之间有着动宾关系。例如：

The object of the "把" sentence must be specific or known by the listener, like "这辆车", "那张报纸", "小王的电脑", etc. In most of the "把" sentences, the object of "把" and the predicate verb of the whole sentence are of verb-object relationship. For example,

③ 小王把那本书卖了。（卖—那本书 V-O）

④ 把门关上。（关—门 V-O）

（5）"把"字句的谓语动词必须是及物动词，要能处置或支配"把"字后面的事物。一些表示视觉、听觉、感觉、知觉的动词，表示存在的动词，关系动词，表示趋向的动词，能愿动词等，没有处置作用，不能用在"把"字句中，比如"觉得、看见、听见、爱、知道、希望、有、在、是、来、去、进来、进去、会"。需要注意的是，"把"字句的谓语动词往往和人体的动作有关，特别是跟"手"的动作有关。例如：

The predicate verb of the "把" sentence must be transitive and can dispose or control the thing after "把". Therefore, those words without the function of disposal cannot be used in the "把" sentence, such as the verbs denoting vision, hearing, feeling or perception, the verbs denoting existence, relationship or direction, or the modal verbs. For instance, "觉得", "看见", "听见", "爱", "知道", "希望", "有", "在", "是", "来", "去", "进来", "进去", and "会", etc. What should be noted is that the predicate verb of the "把" sentence is usually related to a body action, especially to that of hands. For example,

⑤ 我把书有了。（×）

⑥ 他们把教室进去了。（×）

（6）"把" 字句里的谓语成分不能是形容词。例如：

Adjectives cannot be used as the predicate of the "把" sentence. For example,

⑦ 我把衣服脏（zāng, dirty）了。（×）

⑧ 他把衣服弄脏了。（√）

（7）"把" 字句里的谓语动词一般不单独出现，前后要有其他成分，比如：状语 + 动词 + 宾语 / 补语 / "着" / "了"。也可以用动词重叠式。例如：

The predicate verb in the "把" sentence usually does not appear alone. There are other elements both before and after it, such as: adverbial + verb + object / complement / "着" / "了". Reduplication of the verb can also be used. For example,

⑨ 他把手机丢。（×）

⑩ 他把手机丢了。（√）

⑪ 我把汉字写。（×）

⑫ 我把汉字写了三遍。（√）

⑬ 你把你的意见说说。（√）

（8）动态助词 "过" 很少单独用在谓语动词后，如果动词后有表示结果意义的补语，在动补短语后可以用 "过"。

The dynamic auxiliary "过" is seldom used alone after the predicate verb. But if there is a complement of result after the verb, "过" can be put after the verb-complement phrase. For example,

⑭ 老师也把这个字写错过。（√）

3 刚才打了几个喷嚏。I sneezed just now.

"刚才"，名词，表示说话前不久、很短的时间。"刚才" 可以用在动词、形容词或主语前，也可以放在名词前组成 "刚才 + 的 + 名词" 结构。例如：

"刚才", a noun, indicates a short time just before the talk. It can be put before a verb, an adjective or the subject of a sentence. It can also be used before a noun to form the structure "刚才 + 的 +

noun". For example,

　　① 刚才谁来了？

　　② 我已经把刚才的事儿忘了。

辨析 Discrimination　　"刚才"、"刚"

（1）"刚"是副词，作状语，表示动作或情况发生在不久以前。例如：

Serving as the adverbial modifier, "刚", an adverb, indicates that the action or situation happened not long ago. For example,

　　③ 他昨天刚买了一件新衣服。

　　④ 你怎么刚来？

（2）用"刚"的句子末尾不能加"了"，而用"刚才"的句子可以。例如：

The sentence with "刚" cannot end with "了", but the sentence with "刚才" can. For example,

　　⑤ 我刚去游泳了。（×）

　　⑥ 我刚才去游泳了。（√）

（3）"刚"可以组成"刚＋数量词"的结构，但是"刚才"不能。例如：

The word "刚" can be used in the structure "刚 + numeral-measure word", while "刚才" cannot. For example,

　　⑦ 现在刚两点。（√）

　　⑧ 现在刚才两点。（×）

（4）"刚才"可以放在否定词前，而"刚"不行。例如：

"刚才" can be put before the negative word, while "刚" cannot. For example,

　　⑨ 你为什么刚才不同意？（√）

　　⑩ 你为什么刚不同意？（×）

4 　差不多40分钟。**About 40 minutes.**

　　"差不多"，副词，表示相差很少，接近。基本结构：（1）"差不多"＋动词短语／形容词短语，其中常包含数量或程度词语；（2）"差不多"＋数量短语＋名词。例如：

"差不多", an adverb, means "almost" and "nearly" when used in the following structures: (1) "差不多" + verbal phrase / adjectival phrase, usually including the numeral-measure word or the word that denotes degree; (2) 差不多 + numeral-classifier compound + noun. For example,

　　① 他们班差不多有 20 个学生。

　　② 她比我差不多大 10 岁。

　　③ 我们认识了差不多 6 年了。

Nǐ Nǎr Bù Shūfu

你哪儿不舒服

What's wrong with you

3

Kèwén Sān
课文三
Text 3

Lǐ Míngming yě bìng le, tā dào yīyuàn kànbìng.

李明明也病了，她到医院看病。

Li Mingming is also sick and she goes to see the doctor in the hospital.

Yīshēng: Nǐ nǎr bù shūfu?

● 医生：   你哪儿不舒服？

Doctor: What's wrong with you?

Lǐ Míngming: Lā dùzi. Dùzi téngsǐ le!

○ 李明明：   拉肚子。肚子疼死了！

Li Mingming: I have diarrhoea and a bad stomachache.

Yīshēng: Nǐ zuótiān chī shénme le?

● 医生：   你昨天吃什么了？

Doctor: What did you eat yesterday?

Lǐ Míngming: Zuótiān wǎnshang chīle hǎixiān huǒguō, hái hēle hěn duō píjiǔ.

○ 李明明：   昨天晚上吃了海鲜火锅，还喝了很多啤酒。

Li Mingming: I had seafood hotpot and much beer last night.

Yīshēng: Xiān qù huàyàn yíxià ba.
● 医生： 先去化验一下吧。
Doctor: Then take an assay first.

Huàyàn wán yǐhòu, Lǐ Míngming gěi yīshēng kàn huàyàndān.
化验完以后，李明明给医生看化验单。
Li Mingming shows the report of the assay to the doctor after she took the assay.

Yīshēng: Bú tài yánzhòng. Chī diǎnr yào ba.
● 医生： 不太严重。吃点儿药吧。
Doctor: It's not serious. I'll prescribe some medicine for you.

Yīshēng gěi Lǐ Míngming kāile yì zhāng yàofāng.
医生给李明明开了一张药方。
The doctor gives Li Mingming a prescription.

Lǐ Míngming: Zhè yào zěnme chī?
○ 李明明： 这药怎么吃？
Li Mingming: How should I take the medicine?

Yīshēng: Yì tiān liǎng cì, yí cì liǎng piàn. Yào fàn qián chī. Zhùyì duō hē shuǐ,
● 医生： 一天两次，一次两片。要饭前吃。注意多喝水，
duō xiūxi.
多休息。
Doctor: Two pills each time before meals and twice a day. Drink more water and take a good rest.

Lǐ Míngming: Nín gěi wǒ kāi zhāng jiàtiáo ba.
○ 李明明： 您给我开张假条吧。
Li Mingming: Can you give me a note for sick leave?

生词 Shēngcí **New Words**

1. 舒服	shūfu	Adj	comfortable, well
2. 拉肚子	lā dùzi		to suffer from diarrhoea
3. 肚子	dùzi	N	stomach, belly
4. 海鲜	hǎixiān	N	seafood
5. 火锅	huǒguō	N	hotpot
6. 化验	huàyàn	V	to test, to assay
7. 严重	yánzhòng	Adj	serious
8. 片	piàn	M	piece
9. 注意	zhù yì	V//O	to pay attention to
10. 假条	jiàtiáo	N	note asking for leave

注释 Zhùshì **Notes**

1 肚子疼死了！ **I have a bad stomachache.**

不带"得"的程度补语。这时句末一定要有助词"了"。基本结构：主语＋形容词或表示感觉、感情、心理活动的动词＋"极了／多了／死了／坏了／透了"。副词"极"和形容词"多、死、坏、透（tòu，extremely）"与"了"组合之后作程度补语。例如：

This is another form of complement of degree without "得", in which the auxiliary "了" at the end of the sentence is indispensible. The basic structure is "subject + adjective or verb denoting feeling, emotion or mental perception + 极了 / 多了 / 死了／坏了 / 透了". The adverb "极" or the adjective "多", "死", "坏", "透", together with "了", can serve as a complement of degree. For example,

S	Adj / V	Degree Comp
他们俩	讨厌（tǎoyàn, to disgust）	透了。
我	困（kùn, sleepy, tired）	死了。
他	高兴	坏了。

2 一天两次，一次两片。Two pills each time and twice a day.

名词谓语句。这里作主语和谓语的都是数量短语。这类谓语前可以加副词。例如：

It's a noun-predicate sentence in which both subject and predicate are numeral-classifier compounds. An adverb can be added before the predicate. For example,

① 他 30 岁。

② 一本四块八。

③ 一人就一杯。

3 注意多喝水，多休息。Drink more water and take a good rest.

"注意"，动词，意思是把意志放在某一方面。前面可以受"很"等程度副词修饰，后面可以带名词、动词、形容词、小句作宾语。放在句首可以用来表示提醒、命令，或表达关切。也可以单独用来表示提醒。例如：

"注意", a verb, means "to pay attention to…". It can be modified by a degree adverb like "很" before it and can also be followed by a noun, a verb, an adjective, or a clause as the object. When it is used at the beginning of a sentence, it indicates reminding or commanding or expresses a kind of concern. It can also be used alone to indicate reminding. For example,

① 卡尔非常注意锻炼身体。

② 我没注意过他的手上有没有戴表。

③ 注意安全（ānquán, safe）！

④ 注意！

Zhù Tā Zǎorì Kāngfù

祝他早日康复

I hope he will get well soon

Kèwén Sì
课文四
Text 4

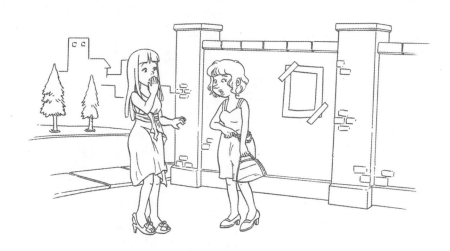

Lǐ Míngming zài lùshang pèngdàole Kāng Àilì, tāmen
tándàole Kǎ'ěr.

李明明在路上碰到了康爱丽，她们谈到了卡尔。

Li Mingming comes across Alice on the road, and they
talk about Karl.

Lǐ Míngming: Àilì, zhè jǐ tiān zěnme méi kànjian Kǎ'ěr? Tā zěnmeyàng?
● 李明明： 爱丽，这几天怎么没看见卡尔？他怎么样？
Li Mingming: Ailce, I haven't seen Karl for several days. How is he?

Kāng Àilì: Tā shàng zhōumò bèi chē zhuàng le.
○ 康爱丽： 他上周末被车撞了。
Alice: He was hit by a car last weekend.

Lǐ Míngming: Shòushāngle ma? Yánzhòng bu yánzhòng?
● 李明明： 受伤了吗？严重不严重？
Li Mingmìng: Was he injured? Was it serious or not?

Kāng Àilì:　Hái suàn xìngyùn. Tā zhǐshì zuǒshǒu gǔzhé le.
○ 康爱丽：　还算幸运。他只是左手骨折了。
Alice:　He was lucky. Only his left hand fractured.

Lǐ Míngming:　Zhùyuànle ma?
● 李明明：　住院了吗？
Li Mingming: Is he in hospital?

Kāng Àilì:　Zhǐ zhùle yì tiān yuàn. Xiànzài zài jiā xiūxi ne.
○ 康爱丽：　只住了一天院。现在在家休息呢。
Alice:　He stayed in hospital only for one day, and now he is having a rest at home.

Lǐ Míngming:　Nà zánmen qù kànkan tā ba.
● 李明明：　那咱们去看看他吧。
Li Mingming: Then let's go to see him.

Kāng Àilì:　Xiànzài? Wǒ děi xiān qù liúxuéshēng bàngōngshì bāng tā qǐngjià.
○ 康爱丽：　现在？我得先去留学生办公室帮他请假。
Alice:　Now? I need to go to the Office of International Students to ask for a leave for him.

Lǐ Míngming:　Qǐngjià děi jiāo yīyuàn de zhěnduàn zhèngmíngshū.
● 李明明：　请假得交医院的诊断证明书。
Li Mingming: Asking for a leave needs the medical certificate from the hospital.

Kāng Àilì:　Yǐjīng kāi le. Nǐ kàn!
○ 康爱丽：　已经开了。你看！
Alice:　I've had it. Look!

Kāng Àilì gěi Lǐ Míngming kàn zhěnduàn zhèngmíngshū.
康爱丽给李明明看诊断证明书。
Alice shows Li Mingming the medical certificate.

Lǐ Míngming:　Nà gǎitiān ba. Wǒ bù zhīdào tā jiā zài nǎr, děng nǐ shénme shíhou
● 李明明：　那改天吧。我不知道他家在哪儿，等你什么时候
yǒu kòngr, péi wǒ qù kàn tā, hǎo ma?
有空儿，陪我去看他，好吗？
Li Mingming: Then we can go to see him another day. I don't know where he lives. Will you go with me when you are free?

Kāng Àilì: Xíng. Wǒ děi zǒu le.

○ 康爱丽: 行。我得走了。

Alice: OK. But I need to go now.

Lǐ Míngming: Qǐng bāng wǒ zhuǎngào tā, zhù tā zǎorì kāngfù!

● 李明明: 请帮我转告他，祝他早日康复！

Li Mingming: Please send my regards to him. I hope he will get well soon!

Kāng Àilì: Hǎo de，méi wèntí.

○ 康爱丽: 好的，没问题。

Alice: OK, no problem.

生词 Shēngcí New Words

1. 祝	zhù	V	to express good wishes, to wish
2. 早日	zǎorì	Adv	early, soon
3. 康复	kāngfù	V	to be restored to health
4. 上	shàng	N	previous, last
5. 被	bèi	Prep	by (expression of passive voice)
6. 撞	zhuàng	V	to bump
7. 受伤	shòu shāng	V//O	to be injured, to be wounded
8. 幸运	xìngyùn	Adj	lucky
9. 只是	zhǐshì	Adv	just, only
10. 左手	zuǒshǒu	N	left hand
11. 骨折	gǔzhé	V	to fracture
12. 住院	zhù yuàn	V//O	to be in hospital
13. 请假	qǐng jià	V//O	to ask for leave
14. 交	jiāo	V	to hand in
15. 诊断证明书	zhěnduàn zhèngmíngshū		medical certificate
16. 陪	péi	V	to accompany
17. 转告	zhuǎngào	V	to send word

注释 Zhùshì Notes

1 他怎么样？ How is he?

"怎么样"，疑问代词，和"怎样"的用法、意思基本相同，用来询问性质、状况和方式等。在句中可以作谓语、状语、补语、宾语、定语。

"怎么样", an interrogative pronoun, with the similar usage and meaning to "怎样", is used to ask about the property, situation or means. It can serve as the predicate, adverbial modifier, complement, object or attribute in a sentence.

辨析 Discrimination "怎么样"、"怎么"

"怎么"，疑问代词，用来询问性质、状况、方式和原因等。

"怎么", an interrogative pronoun, is used to ask about the property, situation, means or reason, etc.

下面通过问句和回答来区别"怎么样"和"怎么"的用法。例如：

Look at the following examples and make a distinction between "怎么样" and "怎么" through some questions and their answers. For example,

	问 Question	答 Answer
作谓语（问状况） Used as the predicate (asking about the situation)	他的电脑怎么了？（√）	坏了。
	他的电脑怎么样？（√）	很好用。
	你看，这件衣服怎么了？（√）	脏了。
	你看，这件衣服怎么样？（√）	不好看。／ 很好看。
	咱们周末去上海，怎么？（×）	
	咱们周末去上海，怎么样？（√）	好的。
	爱丽，你怎么了？（√）	我病了。
	爱丽，你怎么样？（√）	挺好的。
作宾语（问状况） Used as the object (asking about the situation)	请他教我英语，你觉得怎么？（×）	
	请他教我英语，你觉得怎么样？（√）	我觉得很合适。

（续表）

	问 Question	答 Answer
作补语（问状况） Used as the complement (asking about the situation)	他汉语说得怎么？（×）	
	他汉语说得怎么样？（√）	他说得很好。
作定语（问性状） Used as the attribute (asking about the property)	他是怎么一个人？（√）	他挺好的。
	他是怎么样的一个人？（√）	
作状语（问方式） Used as the adverbial (asking about the means)	咱们怎么去？（√）	坐出租车。
	咱们怎么样去？（×）	
	他们怎么吃东西？（√）	他们用筷子吃东西。
	他们怎么样吃东西？（√）	
作状语（问原因） Used as the adverbial (asking about the reason)	你怎么不去上课？（√）	我病了。
	你怎么样不去上课？（×）	

2 他上周末被车撞了。 **He was hit by a car last weekend.**

"被"字句。在谓语动词前由表示被动意义的介词"被"组成的介词短语作状语的句子，叫做"被"字句。包含由表示被动意义的介词"叫、让、给"构成的状语的句子，也属于"被"字句。基本结构：主语＋"被／叫／让／给"＋介词宾语＋谓语动词＋其他成分。例如：

The "被" sentence is a sentence pattern in which the prepositional phrase with the passive marker "被" before the predicate verb serves as the adverbial modifier. "被" can also be substituted by the passive marker "叫", "让" or "给". The basic structure is "subject + 被／叫／让／给 + prepositional object + predicate verb + other elements". For example,

S	A	Prep	O	V	Other elements
他		被	（车）	撞	倒了。
钱包		让	人	偷（tōu, to steal）	了。
书		叫	卡尔	借	走了。
康爱丽		被		派	到中国来了。
他的建议 （jiànyì, suggestion）	已经	被	我们	拒绝。 （jùjué, to refuse）	

（续表）

S	A	Prep	O	V	Other elements
小王	昨天在校外	被		打。	
小王		被		打，	大家都很生气。
小王	没	被		打。	
（1）	（8）	（2）	（3）	（4）（6）（7）	（5）

（1）"被"字句的主语是谓语动词的受事。例如：

The subject of the "被" sentence is the patient of the predicate verb. For example,

① 小王被打了。

（2）在口语中，"叫、让"用得更多，而且多用于一些主语认为是不愉快的事情。

In spoken Chinese, "叫" and "让" are more often used, especially in some unhappy occasions for the subject.

（3）介词"被"的宾语通常是施事。"被"的宾语可以是定指的，也可以是不定指的，还可以省略。不同的是，用介词"叫、让"时，它们的宾语一定要出现。

The object of the preposition "被" is usually the agent and can be either definite or indefinite. It can be omitted sometimes. However, when "叫" or "让" is used, it has to be followed by the object.

（4）"被"字句的谓语动词和"把"字句一样，常常是及物动词。"有、在、是、来、去、回"等动词不能用在"被"字句中。

The same as the "把" sentence, the predicate verb in the "被" sentence is often transitive. The verbs like "有", "在", "是", "来", "去", and "回" cannot be used in the "被" sentence.

注意：能用在"把"字句的动词都能用在"被"字句中，不能用在"被"字句的动词一定不能用在"把"字句中。

Note: The verbs that can be used in the "把" sentence can also be used in the "被" sentence and the verbs that cannot be used in the "被" sentence cannot be used in the "把" sentence, either.

（5）"被"字句表示受事者受到某一动作的作用和影响。和"把"字句一样，"被"字句的谓语一般应该是复杂的形式，不是一个简单的动词，动词一般应该带有状语、宾语、补语或其他成分，动词后要有表示动作完结或结果的成分。动词后的补语可以是结果补语、程度补语、趋向补语、时间补语、动量补语、介词短语补语等。

The "被" sentence indicates that the patient is influenced by an action. The same as the "把" sentence, the predicate of the "被" sentence is usually in a complicated form, not just a simple verb, i.e. the verb is often followed by an adverbial modifier, an object, a complement or other elements to indicate the completion or the result of the action. The complement after the verb can be the complement of result, complement of degree, complement of direction, complement of time, action-measure complement, or complement of the prepositional phrase.

（6）如果谓语动词前有某种状语，介词"被"也有宾语，这时，谓语动词后可以没有其他成分，但是谓语动词不能是单音节的。

If there is an adverbial before the predicate verb and the preposition "被" has its object at the same time, there can be no other element after the predicate verb, but the verb cannot be a monosyllabic one.

（7）当"被"字后面没有宾语时，有些单音节动词也可以作谓语，但前面一般要有状语或者句子后还有后续的内容。

When there is no object following "被", some monosyllabic verbs can serve as the predicate, but there is usually an adverbial modifier before it or some follow-up elements in the latter half of the sentence.

（8）如果有否定副词"没"或能愿动词"要"，"没"和"要"应放在"被"的前面。例如：

If the negative adverb "没" or modal verb "要" is used in the sentence, they should be put before "被". For example,

② 钱没被我花完。（ √ ）
③ 钱被我没花完。（ × ）
④ 蛋糕要被他吃完了。（ √ ）
⑤ 蛋糕被要他吃完了。（ × ）

3 他只是左手骨折了。Only his left hand fractured.

"只是"，副词，意思是"仅仅是，不过是"，表示限定范围，说明除此之外没有别的情况。可以作状语。例如：

"只是", an adverb, means "only", indicating a limited scope, i.e. there is nothing else but what is said. It can be used as an adverbial modifier. For example,

① 他只是点了点头，没说话。
② 我们只是去逛了逛王府井，没去别的地方。
③ A：你怎么了？哪儿不舒服？
　　B：我只是有点儿累。

4 我得先去留学生办公室帮他请假。

I need to go to the Office of International Students to ask for a leave for him.

连动句。谓语由两个或两个以上的动词构成，在动词短语中间没有停顿，也没有关联词语，两个动词短语共用一个主语，这样的句子叫连动句。本句是三个动词短语连用："去留学生办公室"、"帮他"、"请假"。状语、否定副词"不"或"没（有）"要放在第一个谓语动词前面。例如：

This is a serial-verb sentence, i.e. a sentence which has two or more predicate verbs sharing one subject without any pause or conjunctive in between. There are three verbal phrases in this sentence: "去留学生办公室", "帮他", and "请假". The adverbial modifier or negative adverb "不" or "没（有）" should be put before the first predicate verb. For example,

① 她坐公共汽车去超市买菜。

② 明明也去医院看病。

③ 他没去机场接他的朋友。

5 祝他早日康复！I hope he will get well soon!

"祝"，动词，意思是"祝愿"。放在句首，常用来表示良好的愿望和祝福。如人们常对生病的人说"祝您早日康复"。再如：

"祝", a verb, meaning "to wish", is used at the beginning of a sentence to express one's good wishes or blessing. In Chinese, "祝您早日康复" is often said to patients. For example,

① 祝您（身体）健康！

② 祝大家新年快乐！

③ 祝你一路平安！

④ 祝你成功！

练习　Liànxí　**Exercises**

一　跟读生词，注意发音和声调。
Read the new words after the teacher and pay attention to your pronunciation and tones.

二　跟读课文，注意语音语调。
Read the texts after the teacher and pay attention to your pronunciation and intonation.

三　学生分组，分角色朗读课文一、二。
Divide the students into groups and read Texts 1 & 2 in different roles.

四　学生分组，不看书，分角色表演课文一、二。
Divide the students into groups and play the roles in Texts 1 & 2 without referring to the book.

五　角色扮演。（提示：角色可以互换。）
Role playing. (Note: the roles can be exchanged.)

1. 如果你看见朋友不舒服，你会怎么说？请就这个话题，用下面的词语和句子完成一段对话。
Suppose you find your friend is not feeling well. What do you say to him? Make a dialogue with the following words and sentences on this topic.

你怎么了？／你哪儿不舒服？／你怎么不舒服？

陪你看大夫／挂号／吃药／注意……

2. 两人一组，一人扮演病人，一人扮演医生，表演看病的情景。
Work in pairs: one as the patient and the other as the doctor. Make a dialogue.

六　复述课文二和课文四。
Retell Texts 2 & 4.

七 替换练习。
Substitution drills.

① 我 疼 得 厉害。

我		难受	要死
我		累	要命
她的脸		红	很
今天的菜		好吃	不得了

② 38 ℃，不 算 高。

这个问题		你答对了
他		是好学生
这几个	就	5 块钱吧
今天	不	冷

③ 把 嘴 张开。

这张桌子	放在中间
车	停在门口
空调	关上
合同	签了
眼睛	闭上

④ 你感冒了，不过 不厉害。

这家酒店很贵	离机场很近
我们公司有点儿远	坐地铁上班很方便
他很爱我	我不爱他
促销的产品很（chǎnpǐn, product）多	有的质量（zhìliàng, quality）不好

⑤ <u>一天</u>　<u>两次</u>。

二月	28 天
这座楼	3 层
这个菜	7 块
一个盘子（pánzi, plate）里	一块点心（diǎnxin, dim sum）

⑥ 注意　<u>多喝水，多休息</u>。

听老师讲课
你的钱包
每天都要吃药
这儿

⑦ <u>卡尔</u>　被　<u>车</u>　<u>撞了</u>。

我的手机	人	偷走了
碗里的肉	他的狗	吃了
他的钱	老婆（lǎopo, wife）	拿走了
我	老板	骂（mà, to scold）了

⑧ 他　只是　<u>左手骨折了</u>。

心情不太好
头疼
身体有点儿不舒服
嗓子有点儿难受

⑨ 等　你什么时候有空儿，　陪我去看他。

我有钱了	请你吃饭
你放假了	我们一起去旅游吧
你们见了面	你就会喜欢她的
你下了课	我们再去超市

八　用下面的词语组成句子。
Make sentences with the following words and expressions.

① 你　内科．门诊部　可以　挂　在

② 个　病历本　的　买　时候　挂号　要

③ 先　你　体温　一下　量　去

④ 喷嚏　了　几　打　刚才　个

⑤ 先　开　给你　吧　药　点儿

⑥ 出差　后天　要　我

⑦ 输　得　那　时间　多长

⑧ 了　肚子　死　疼

⑨ 先去　帮他　得　留学生办公室　请假　我

⑩ 陪我　他　好吗　看　去　你

九 用"把"完成下面的句子。
Complete the sentences with "把".

Example：我　作业　做 ——→ 我把作业做完了。

❶ 书　　放　　书包 ——→

❷ 明明　　照片　　寄　　妈妈 ——→

❸ 卡尔　　美元　　换　　人民币 ——→

❹ 她　　电脑　　关 ——→

❺ 你的想法　　说 ——→

❻ 我　　作业　　交给　　老师（否定式）——→

❼ 他　　能　　意见　　告诉我（否定式）——→

十 用"被"完成下面的句子。
Complete the sentences with "被".

Example：点心　我　吃 ——→ 点心被我吃完了。

❶ 他　　坏人　　打 ——→

❷ 东西　　小张　　拿 ——→

❸ 汽车　　朋友　　开 ——→

❹ 她奶奶　　送到　　医院 ——→

❺ 他的申请　　已经　　学校　　批准 ——→

⑥ 他的车　　借（否定式）——→

十一　完成下面的对话。
Complete the dialogues.

① A：你怎么了？哪儿不舒服？

B：我_____。

A：我陪你去看看吧。

② A：_____？

B：好的。给你书。

③ A：刚才我去找你。你不在。你去哪儿了？

B：_____。

④ A：你们公司有多少人？

B：_____。

⑤ A：张明_____？

B：老师，他刚给我发短信，说他病了。

⑥ A：听说你去年去中国了？

B：对，我_____工作了一年，刚刚回国。（派）

A：中国_____？

B：中国现在发展（fāzhǎn, to develop）很快，很多国家都把中国当做
（dàngzuò, to treat as, to regard as）最大的市场。

⑦ A：于经理，_____？

B：好。回家好好休息吧。

十二　扩展练习。
Extended exercises.

1. 对病人的建议　Giving suggestions to patients

	B：你去看病吧。
A：我病了。	看大夫
	看中医（zhōngyī, traditional Chinese medicine）
	看西医（xīyī, Western medicine）

2. 挂号时 At the registration office

A：挂什么？	B：挂一个内科。
	内科专家号
	外科普通号

3. 去医院咨询挂号时 At the information desk in a hospital

A：我头疼，挂什么科？	B：挂内科。
感冒了（流鼻涕、打喷嚏、嗓子疼、发烧）	内科
眼睛不舒服	眼科
手破（pò, to break）了	外科
腿断（duàn, to break off）了	外科
肚子疼	内科
胃（wèi, stomach）疼	内科

十三 阅读理解。
Reading comprehension.

　　中医是中国的国粹，有些中国人生病以后，常常会选择看中医。以前，很多西方人不了解中国的历史和文化，不能接受中医。现在，很多国家都开始应用中医的方法治病。今天，在瑞典的医院里，医生会问产妇，是不是希望用针灸来减轻生孩子时的疼痛感。有一家西方的医药公司，已经成功地研发出含有中药成分的西药，这种药可治疗哮喘病。美国的科学家还证明，一些中药中的物质对酗酒者有疗效。这些也算是中医药的发展。

生词　Shēngcí　**New Words**

1. 国粹	guócuì	N	the quintessence of a country
2. 有些	yǒuxiē	Pr	some
3. 了解	liǎojiě	V	to know
4. 接受	jiēshòu	V	to accept

5. 应用	yìngyòng	V	to apply
6. 瑞典	Ruìdiǎn	PN	Sweden
7. 产妇	chǎnfù	N	lying-in woman
8. 针灸	zhēnjiǔ	N	acupuncture and moxibustion
9. 减轻	jiǎnqīng	V	to lighten
10. 成功	chénggōng	Adj	successful
11. 研发	yánfā	V	to research and develop
12. 含	hán	V	to comprise
13. 成分	chéngfèn	N	component
14. 治疗	zhìliáo	V	to treat
15. 哮喘	xiàochuǎn	N	asthma
16. 科学家	kēxuéjiā	N	scientist
17. 证明	zhèngmíng	V	to prove
18. 物质	wùzhì	N	matter
19. 酗酒者	xùjiǔzhě	N	sot
20. 疗效	liáoxiào	N	curative effect

1. 回答问题：

Answer the questions:

① 有些中国人生病以后，常常会怎么做？

② 以前西方人对中医怎么看？

③ 在瑞典的医院里，医生会问产妇什么？

④ 那家西方的医药公司研发出了什么药？这种药可以治疗什么病？

⑤ 美国科学家证明了什么？

2. 思考并表达：

Think and express:

看了这篇短文后你有什么想法？你们国家有没有中医？你认识的人对中医的看法是什么？你对中医的看法是什么？

3. 辩论：

Discussion:

正方：Positive side:

我接受中医为我看病

反方：Negative side:

我不接受中医为我看病

十四 完成任务：请用课文中学过的词语和句子完成任务。

Complete the tasks: Please complete the tasks with the words and sentences you have learned in the texts.

1. 去附近的医院了解看病的流程，然后在课堂上向老师和同学介绍。

Go to the hospital nearby to get to know the procedure of seeing the doctor, and present the information you get to your teacher and classmates in class.

2. 向你认识的中国人了解看望病人需要注意的地方，包括：

Ask your Chinese friends about what should be paid attention to when visiting a patient, including:

(1) 在医院的病房里或病人的家里应该注意什么？

What should be paid attention to in the ward of the hospital or at the patient's home?

(2) 送礼物应该注意什么？

What should be paid attention to when giving presents?

(3) 说话时应该注意什么？什么可以说？什么不能说？

What should be paid attention to when speaking? What can be said? What cannot be said?

了解清楚后，请到课堂上向老师和同学介绍，然后大家一起讨论中国在这方面的习惯和你们国家有什么不同。

After collecting all of the above information, present it to your teacher and classmates in class, and discuss with them about in which ways China is different from your own country in this aspect.

第十二单元
UNIT **12**
租房
Renting an apartment

你打算租什么样的房子
What kind of apartment
do you want to rent

课文 Text	题目 Title	注释 Notes
一	你打算租什么样的房子 What kind of apartment do you want to rent	1. 叹词"嘿"　The interjection "嘿" 2. 副词"一直"　The adverb "一直" 3. 副词"最好"　The adverb "最好" 4. 表示假设关系的复句:"如果……,就……"(复习) The compound sentence denoting a suppositional relation "如果……,就……" (Review) 5. 指示代词"有的" The demonstrative pronoun "有的" 6. 单音节形容词的重叠 The reduplicate form of a monosyllabic adjective 7. 兼语句　The pivotal sentence 8. 表示让步关系的复句:"A 倒是 A,可是 B" The compound sentence denoting concession: "A 倒是 A, 可是 B" 9. "想起来了" 10. 动词"拜托"　The verb "拜托"
二	一平米一天多少钱呢 What's the rent for one square meter per day	1. "我想问一下" 2. "多 + 长 / 大 / 重 / 高" 3. 主谓谓语句(复习) The subject-predicate predicate sentence (Review) 4. 用"有没有"的正反疑问句 The affirmative-negative question with "有没有" 5. 动词"过来"(复习)　The verb "过来" (Review)

| 三 | 康爱丽的办公室
Alice's office | 1. 转折复句："虽然……，但是……"
The transitional compound sentence "虽然……，但是……"
2. 动态助词"着"及存在句
The aspect particle "着" and the existential sentence |

Nǐ Dǎsuàn Zū Shénmeyàng de Fángzi
你打算租什么样的房子
What kind of apartment do you want to rent

Lǐ Míngming zài xiàoyuán li pèngdàole Kǎ'ěr.
李明明在校园里碰到了卡尔。
Li Mingming runs into Karl on the campus.

Lǐ Míngming: Hēi, Kǎ'ěr!
● 李明明：　　嘿，卡尔！
Li Mingming: Hi, Karl!

Kǎ'ěr:　　　 Hēi, Míngming!
○ 卡尔：　　　嘿，明明！
Karl:　　　　Hi, Mingming!

Lǐ Míngming: Zuìjìn máng shénme ne?
● 李明明：　　最近忙什么呢？
Li Mingming: What's up?

Kǎ'ěr:　　　 Yìzhí zài zhǎo fángzi ne.
○ 卡尔：　　　一直在找房子呢。
Karl:　　　　I am looking for an apartment.

Lǐ Míngming: Nǐ xiǎng bān chuqu? Zěnmeyàng le?
● 李明明: 你想搬出去？怎么样了？
Li Mingming: You want to move out? Have you found one?

Kǎ'ěr: Zhèng fāchóu ne, hái méiyǒu zhǎodào héshì de.
○ 卡尔: 正发愁呢，还没有找到合适的。
Karl: It really bothers me. I haven't found a suitable one yet.

Lǐ Míngming: Nǐ dǎsuàn zū shénmeyàng de fángzi?
● 李明明: 你打算租什么样的房子？
Li Mingming: What kind of apartment do you want to rent?

Kǎ'ěr: Wǒ xiǎng zū yí tào liǎng jūshì. Wèishēngjiān hé chúfáng yídìng yào
○ 卡尔: 我想租一套两居室。卫生间和厨房一定要
gānjìng, kètīng zuìhǎo dà yìdiǎnr. Rúguǒ wòshì yǒu yángtái,
干净，客厅最好大一点儿。如果卧室有阳台，
nà jiù gèng hǎo le.
那就更好了。
Karl: I want a suite with two bedrooms. The bathroom and the kitchen should be clean, and the living room should be large. It will be better if there is a balcony in the bedroom.

Lǐ Míngming: Zhèyàng de fángzi tǐng duō de ba? Yīnggāi bú tài nán zhǎo.
● 李明明: 这样的房子挺多的吧？应该不太难找。
Li Miming: There are lots of such apartments. It shouldn't be too difficult to find one.

Kǎ'ěr: Fángzi dàoshì tǐng duō de, kěshì, yǒude lí xuéxiào tài yuǎn, yǒude
○ 卡尔: 房子倒是挺多的，可是，有的离学校太远，有的
kàojìn mǎlù, hái yǒude ne, fángzū tài gāo le. Zhēn máfan!
靠近马路，还有的呢，房租太高了。真麻烦！
Karl: There are a lot indeed. But some are too far away from the school, some are too close to the streets, and some others are too expensive. It's really troublesome.

Lǐ Míngming: Bié zháojí, mànmàn zhǎo ba. Duì le, wǒ de yí ge péngyou ràng
● 李明明: 别着急，慢慢找吧。对了，我的一个朋友让
zhōngjiè gōngsī bāng tā zūle yí tào fángzi. Shěngshì dàoshì tǐng
中介公司帮她租了一套房子。省事倒是挺
shěngshì de, kěshì tā děi fù zhōngjièfèi.
省事的，可是她得付中介费。

Li Mingming: Don't worry, and take it easy. Oh, one of my friends has found an apartment with the help of an agency. It indeed saved her a lot of trouble, but she needed to pay the agency.

Kǎ'ěr: Zhōngjiè gōngsī? Wǒ juéde gèng máfan. Háishi zìjǐ zhǎo ba.
○ 卡尔：   中介公司？我觉得更麻烦。还是自己找吧。
Karl: Agency? It's more troublesome. I would rather find one by myself.

Lǐ Míngming: Xiǎng qilai le, qiántiān wǒ qù péngyou jiā, tāmen lóu shàng yǒu
● 李明明：   想起来了，前天我去朋友家，他们楼上有
           rén zài lóudào li tiēle guǎnggào, xiǎng chūzū fángzi.
           人在楼道里贴了广告，想出租房子。
Li Mingming: I remember it. When I went to one of my friends' home the day before yesterday, I saw an advertisement about apartment renting put up on the corridor in the building.

Kǎ'ěr: Nàge xiǎoqū zài nǎr?
○ 卡尔：   那个小区在哪儿？
Karl: Where is the community?

Lǐ Míngming: Jiù zài zánmen xuéxiào fùjìn. Xiǎoqū huánjìng búcuò, érqiě yǒu
● 李明明：   就在咱们学校附近。小区环境不错，而且有
           chāoshì、càishìchǎng、xǐyīdiàn、yóujú、yòu'éryuán, fēicháng
           超市、菜市场、洗衣店、邮局、幼儿园，非常
           fāngbiàn. Wǒ bāng nǐ wènwen.
           方便。我帮你问问。
Li Mingming: It's just near our school. The environment is very good, and there is a supermarket, a food market, a laundry, a post office, and a kindergarten nearby. It's very convenient. I can ask about it for you.

Kǎ'ěr: Nà jiù bàituō nǐ le.
○ 卡尔：   那就拜托你了。
Karl: Thanks for your help.

Lǐ Míngming: Bú kèqi!
● 李明明：   不客气！
Li Mingming: You're welcome.

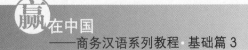

Fù: Kǎ'ěr de Qiú Zū Guǎnggào

附：卡尔的求租广告

Attached: Apartment wanted advertisement

Qiú   Zū
求　租
Apartment Wanted

Běnrén xiǎng zài Jīngmào Dàxué fùjìn zū yí tào liǎng jūshì de fángzi.

本人想在经贸大学附近租一套两居室的房子。

I want to rent an apartment with two bedrooms near the University of International Business and Economics.

Yāoqiú: Wèishēngjiān hé chúfáng yào gānjìng, kètīng zuìhǎo dà yìdiǎnr,

要求：卫生间和厨房要干净，客厅最好大一点儿，

wòshì zuìhǎo yǒu yángtái.

卧室最好有阳台。

Requirements: The bathroom and the kitchen should be clean, and the living room should be large. It will be better if there is a balcony in the bedroom.

Yǒuyìzhě qǐng yǔ běnrén liánxì, shǒujī: yāo sān sān bā bā liù liù sān wǔ qī líng.

有意者请与本人联系，手机：13388663570。

Zhōngjiè wù rǎo.

中介勿扰。

Please contact me if you have the right apartment. My phone: 13388663570. Please do not bother if you are an agent.

生词 Shēngcí **New Words**

1. 租	zū	V	to rent
2. 嘿	hēi	Int	Hi
3. 一直	yìzhí	Adv	always
4. 发愁	fā chóu	V//O	to be worried
5. 套	tào	M	*a measure word*
6. 两居室	liǎng jūshì		an apartment with two bedrooms
7. 卫生间	wèishēngjiān	N	washroom
8. 厨房	chúfáng	N	kitchen
9. 一定	yídìng	Adv	must, surely, certainly
10. 干净	gānjìng	Adj	clean
11. 客厅	kètīng	N	living room
12. 最好	zuìhǎo	Adv	had better
13. 如果	rúguǒ	Conj	if, in case
14. 卧室	wòshì	N	bedroom
15. 阳台	yángtái	N	balcony
16. 有的	yǒude	Pr	some
17. 靠近	kàojìn	V	to get near, to approach
18. 房租	fángzū	N	rent
19. 麻烦	máfan	Adj	troublesome
20. 着急	zháo jí	V//O	to get worried
21. 慢	màn	Adj	slow
22. 中介	zhōngjiè	N	intermediary, agent
23. 省事	shěngshì	Adj	convenient
24. 倒是	dàoshì	Adv	*used to indicate concession*
25. 付	fù	V	to pay
26. 前天	qiántiān	N	the day before yesterday

27. 楼道	lóudào	N	corridor
28. 贴	tiē	V	to paste or stick on
29. 广告	guǎnggào	N	advertisement
30. 出租	chūzū	V	to rent out
31. 小区	xiǎoqū	N	residential area
32. 菜市场	càishìchǎng	N	food market
33. 洗衣店	xǐyīdiàn	N	laundry
34. 邮局	yóujú	N	post office
35. 幼儿园	yòu'éryuán	N	kindergarten
36. 拜托	bàituō	V	to request a favour

注释　Zhùshì　**Notes**

1　嘿，卡尔！Hi, Karl! / 嘿，明明！Hi, Mingming!

"嘿"，叹词，表示招呼和引起注意。口语中，人们打招呼可以互相说"嘿"，尤其是年轻人之间。"嘿"相当于英语中的"Hi"。

"嘿", an exclamation, is used to arouse others' attention. In spoken Chinese, people, especially the young, often greet each other with "嘿". It is the equivalent of "Hi" in English.

2　一直在找房子呢。I am looking for an apartment.

"一直"，副词，放在谓语前，作状语，可以用来表示动作始终不间断或者状态始终不变，前面常常可以加上表示一段时间的词语，如"最近、这段（zhè duàn, this period of time）时间、这几天"等。例如：

"一直", an adverb, is usually put before the predicate as the adverbial modifier. It can be used to indicate that an action is lasting or a state has not changed all the time. A word or phrase denoting a period of time, such as "最近", "这段时间" or "这几天", is often added before it. For example,

S	P		
	Time period	Adv（一直）	V +O / Adj
他	最近		在找工作。
卡尔	这段时间	一直	很忙。
我	这两年		在国外。

3 客厅最好大一点儿。The living room should be large.

"最好"，副词。当句子的主语是事物时，"最好"表示它后面提出来的是最理想的状态或者最合适的方式等。例如：

"最好" is an adverb. When the subject of the sentence is a thing, the part after "最好" denotes the ideal state or most suitable way. For example,

① 这封信最好用英文写。

② 苹果最好是新鲜（xīnxiān, fresh）的。

当主语是人时，"最好"常常表示给出建议，语气委婉，不是直接让别人做什么，也不是强迫别人接受。例如：

When the subject is a person, "最好" is used to give suggestions in a mild tone, not to make others do something or force others to accept something. For example,

③ 你最好去看医生。

④ 你最好打电话问问。

4 如果卧室有阳台，那就更好了。 It will be better if there is a balcony in the bedroom.

"如果……，就……"，表示假设关系的复句。复句，指两个或两个以上在意义上有关系的单句组成的一个能表达完整意思的句子。复句中的单句叫分句。假设复句是前一分句提出一个假设的情况，后一分句表示由假设情况产生的结果或推论。前一分句常用连词"如果、要是（yàoshi, if）"，后一分句常用副词"就"。当前一分句和后一分句主语相同时，主语放在前一分句，可以放在"如果"之前，也可以放在"如果"之后。例如：

"如果……，就……" is a compound sentence denoting a suppositional relation. The compound sentence is a sentence in which two or more semantically related simple sentences express a complete meaning. Each simple sentence is a "clause". In spoken Chinese, if we want to denote a suppositional relation, we can use "就" in the latter clause and "如果" or "要是" in the first clause. When the two clauses A and B share the same subject, the subject can be put either before or after "如果" in the first clause. For example,

clause 1			clause 2	
Conj（如果、要是）	S	P₁	Adv（就）	P₂
如果（要是）	房租	能便宜点儿，	就	好了。
	房子附近	有菜市场，		更方便了。

也可以像下面这样：

It can also be like this:

clause 1			clause 2	
S	Conj（如果、要是）	P₁	Adv（就）	P₂
房租	如果（要是）	能便宜点儿，	就	好了。
房子附近		有菜市场，		更方便了。

当前后两个分句的主语不同时，第一个主语放在"如果"之后，第二个主语放在"就"之前。例如：

When the subjects of the two clauses are different, the first subject is put after "如果" and the second one before "就". For example,

clause 1				clause 2	
Conj（如果）	S₁	P₁	S₂	Adv（就）	P₂
如果	小区附近	有菜市场，	我	就	租这里的房子。
	他	还不来，	我们		走吧。

5 **房子倒是挺多的，可是，有的离学校太远，有的靠近马路，还有的呢，房租太高了。**

There are a lot indeed. But some are too far away from the school, some are too close to the streets, and some others are too expensive.

"有的"，指示代词，表示人或事物中的一部分。常常两个或两个以上连用，分类别来说明不同的人或者事物，前面也常有表示人或事物所在的整体的词语。有时可以在最后一个前面加上副词"还"，表示在已有情况上的增补，范围扩大。例如：

"有的", a pronoun, indicates a part of people or things. It is usually used twice or more times in a sentence and sometimes the adverb "还" is added before the last one to indicate there is an additional one besides the ones listed before or the scope is increased. This structure is used to illustrate different people or things separately. A word indicating the whole to which the specific people or things belong is often used before the structure. For example,

① 他们有的是英国（Yīngguó, Britain）人，有的是美国人，还有的是德国人。

② 同学们有的唱歌，有的跳舞。

6 别着急，慢慢找吧。Don't worry, and take it easy.

"慢慢"，单音节形容词的重叠。一部分单音节形容词 A 可以重叠为 AA。形容词重叠后程度加强了，或者有了某种感情色彩，有了描写的作用。本句中"慢慢"的程度比"慢"高一些。形容词重叠式常常放在动词的前面，表示动作所处的状态。例如：

The reduplicate form of a monosyllabic adjective is AA. Some of the adjective could be reduplicated. After the reduplication of the adjective, the degree expressed is reinforced or the sentence is endued with a kind of feeling. "慢慢" here is higher than "慢" in degree. The reduplicate form is often put before a verb, indicating the state of the action. For example,

A	AA	例 Examples
好	好好	你要好好学习。
轻（qīng，light）	轻轻	他轻轻地走进教室。
慢	慢慢	车慢慢停了下来。

7 我的一个朋友让中介公司帮她租了一套房子。

One of my friends has found an apartment with the help of an agency.

兼语句。兼语句的谓语是由一个动宾短语和一个主谓短语组合在一起构成的，谓语部分的前一个动宾短语的宾语兼作后一个主谓短语的主语。基本结构：

This is a pivotal sentence. The predicate of the pivotal sentence is composed of a verb-object phrase and a subject-predicate phrase, and the object of the verb-object phrase is the subject of the subject-predicate phrase. The basic structure is:

S_1	P_1			
	V_1	$\leftarrow O_1$ $(S_2)\rightarrow$	P_2	
			V_2	O_2

本句中的"中介公司"既是前面动词"让"的宾语，又是后面"帮她租了一套房子"的主语。

In this sentence, "中介公司" is both the object of the verb "让" and the subject of "帮她租了一套房子", so it is a linkage.

兼语句的第一个动词常常是"让、叫、请"等表示使令意义的动词，这时兼语后面的词语所表示的动作或状态是第一个动词所表示的动作引起的。兼语句的第一个动词也可以是"有/没有"，这时兼语表示存在的人或事物。例如：

The first verb of a pivotal sentence is always causative in meaning, such as "让", "叫", or "请", etc, and the action or state expressed by the words after the linkage is caused by the action expressed by the first verb. When the first verb of the pivotal sentence is "有/没有", the linkage denotes the existing people or things. For example,

S_1	V_1	O_1 / S_2	V_2	O_2
我	让	他	帮	你 (问问)。
卡尔	请	我	吃	饭。
妈妈	叫	我	买	五斤苹果。
他们楼上	有	人	贴了	广告。

8 省事倒是挺省事的，可是她得付中介费。

It indeed saved her a lot of trouble, but she needed to pay the agency.

"A 倒是 A，可是 B"，表示让步关系的复句。在这一结构中，副词"倒是"用在前一分句中肯定某种事实，作出让步，后一分句中常常用"可是、但是、不过、就是"从相反的方面引出说话者想说的情况。根据说话人的需要，也可以用"A 倒是不 A，可是 B"。A 是相同的动词或形容词，B 可以是主谓短语、动宾短语、形容词短语等。例如：

"A 倒是 A, 可是 B" is a compound sentence denoting concession. In this structure, the adverb "倒是" is used in the first clause to confirm a truth, indicating a kind of concession. "可是", "但是", "不过", or "就是" is often used in the latter clause to bring out the opposite situation the speaker wants to talk about. Based on the speaker's need, the structure "A 倒是不 A，可是 B" can also be used. A is a verb or an adjective, and B can be a subject-predicate phrase, a verb-object phrase, or an adjective phrase, etc. For example,

sth. / sb.	A	倒是	（不）A	可是 / 但是 / 不过 / 就是	B
房租	便宜		便宜，	不过	卫生间太小了。
小区的环境	好		好，	可是	附近没有车站。
这课的生词	难	倒是	不难，	就是	太多了。
他	坏		不坏，	就是	有点儿小气（xiǎoqi, stingy, mean）。

9　想起来了。　I remember it.

"想起来了"，用在句首，常常用来表示说话人忽然想到了之前忘了的事情。"想"，这里不是以前学的能愿动词"希望、打算"的意思，而是动词"动脑筋、思索"的意思，可以单独作谓语。"起来"是趋向动词，放在动词后，组成"动词＋（不）起来＋了"的结构。这里的"起来"不表示动作由下向上，而是表示动作完成或是达到了一定的目的、结果。

Put at the beginning of a sentence, "想起来了" indicates that the speaker suddenly remembers something. "想" here means "to remember, to think", similar to "动脑筋, 思索", which is different from the optative verbs "希望" and "打算" we have learned before. It can serve as the predicate by itself. "起来", a directional verb, is often put after another verb to form the structure "verb ＋（不）起来 ＋ 了". "起来" here indicates that the action is finished or the goal is reached.

10　那就拜托你了。Thanks for your help.

"拜托"，动词，敬辞。请别人帮忙做某事时常说，也可以单说。例如：

"拜托", a verb, is a term of respect. It is often used when we ask others for a favor, and can be used alone. For example,

① 我身体不舒服，拜托你告诉老师。

② 我要去机场接我的朋友，拜托你帮我请假。

③ 这是我给他的生日礼物，拜托您带给他。

④ 请您多帮帮这个孩子，拜托了！

Yì Píngmǐ Yì Tiān Duōshao Qián

一平米一天多少钱

What's the rent for one square meter per day

Kāng Àilì xiǎng zū xiězìlóu, tā de mìshū Xiǎo Qián gěi Lántiān Dàshà Zūshòubù dǎ diànhuà.

康爱丽想租写字楼,她的秘书小钱给蓝天大厦租售部打电话。

Alice wants to rent an office room, and Xiao Qian, her secretary, gives a call to the Rental and Sales Department of the Blue Sky Tower.

Xiǎo Qián:　　Nǐ hǎo! Shì Lántiān Dàshà Zūshòubù ma?

● 小钱：　　你好！是蓝天大厦租售部吗?

Xiao Qian:　　Hello. Is that the Rental and Sales Department of the Blue Sky Tower?

Wáng jīnglǐ:　　Duì. Nín shì nǎ wèi?

○ 王经理：　　对。您是哪位?

Manager Wang: Yes. Who is calling?

Xiǎo Qián:
● 小钱：　Wǒ xìng Qián. Wǒ xiǎng wèn yíxià, nǐmen dàshà hái yǒu xiězìlóu
我姓钱。我想问一下，你们大厦还有写字楼
chūzū ma?
出租吗？

Xiao Qian:　My surname is Qian. Excuse me, are there still any office rooms available for renting?

Wáng jīnglǐ:
○ 王经理：　Yǒu. Nǐmen xiǎng zū duō dà miànjī de?
有。你们想租多大面积的？
Manager Wang: Yes, there are. How large a room do you want?

Xiǎo Qián:
● 小钱：　Èrbǎi píngmǐ zuǒyòu. Yì píngmǐ yì tiān duōshao qián?
200平米左右。一平米一天多少钱？
Xiao Qian:　Around 200 square meters. What's the rent for one square meter per day?

Wáng jīnglǐ:
○ 王经理：　Wǔ kuài. Èrbǎi píngmǐ yí ge yuè sānwàn zuǒyòu.
5块。200平米一个月3万左右。
Manager Wang: Five *kuai*. 30,000 *yuan* for a month in all.

Xiǎo Qián:
● 小钱：　Bāokuò wùyèfèi hé tíngchēfèi ma?
包括物业费和停车费吗？
Xiao Qian:　Including property management charge and parking fee?

Wáng jīnglǐ:
○ 王经理：　Bāokuò wùyèfèi, búguò chēwèi lìngwài shōu fèi. Hái yǒu, diànfèi
包括物业费，不过车位另外收费。还有，电费
zìjǐ fù.
自己付。
Manager Wang: The property management charge is included, but the charges for electricity and parking are not.

Xiǎo Qián:
● 小钱：　Chēwèi yí ge yuè duōshao qián?
车位一个月多少钱？
Xiao Qian:　How much is one parking space per month?

Wáng jīnglǐ:
○ 王经理：　Dìshàng chēwèi yí ge yuè liùbǎi kuài, dìxià chēwèi yí ge yuè
地上车位一个月600块，地下车位一个月
yìqiān kuài.
1000块。
Manager Wang: 600 *kuai* per month for each parking space on the ground, and 1000 *kuai* per month for each underground.

Xiǎo Qián: Yǒudiǎnr guì. Yǒu méiyǒu miǎnzūqī?

● 小钱：   有点儿贵。有没有免租期？

Xiao Qian: It's a little expensive. Is there a rent-free period?

Wáng jīnglǐ: Rúguǒ nín qiānle hétong, wǒmen jiù kěyǐ gěi nín èrshí tiān de

○ 王经理：   如果您签了合同，我们就可以给您 20 天的

zhuāngxiū shíjiān.

装修时间。

Manager Wang: If you sign the contract, we can give you a rent-free period of 20 days

for interior decoration.

Xiǎo Qián: Hǎo de, wǒ děi gēn lǎobǎn shāngliang yíxià. Xièxie nín!

● 小钱：   好的，我得跟老板商量一下。谢谢您！

Xiao Qian: Ok. I need to discuss with my boss. Thank you!

Wáng jīnglǐ: Bú kèqi, nín suíshí kěyǐ guòlai kàn fáng.

○ 王经理：   不客气，您随时可以过来看房。

Manager Wang: You are welcome. You can come to take a look at any time.

Xiǎo Qián: Hǎo de, zàijiàn!

● 小钱：   好的，再见！

Xiao Qian: All right. Goodbye!

Wáng jīnglǐ: Zàijiàn!

○ 王经理：   再见！

Manager Wang: Goodbye!

生词 Shēngcí New Words

1. 平米	píngmǐ	N	square meter
2. 租售部	zūshòubù	N	rental and sales department
3. 大厦	dàshà	N	building, edifice
4. 写字楼	xiězìlóu	N	office building
5. 面积	miànjī	N	area
6. 万	wàn	M	ten thousand
7. 包括	bāokuò	V	to consist of, to include

8.	物业	wùyè	N	property
9.	停车	tíng chē	V//O	to park
10.	车位	chēwèi	N	parking space
11.	另外	lìngwài	Adv	in addition, besides
12.	收	shōu	V	to gain (economic benefits)
13.	电	diàn	N	electricity
14.	自己	zìjǐ	Pr	oneself
15.	地上	dìshàng	N	on the ground
16.	地下	dìxià	N	underground
17.	免租期	miǎnzūqī	N	rent-free period
18.	签	qiān	V	to sign
19.	合同	hétong	N	contract
20.	装修	zhuāngxiū	V	to decorate, to renovate
21.	商量	shāngliang	V	to discuss
22.	随时	suíshí	Adv	at any time

专有名词 Zhuānyǒu Míngcí **Proper Nouns**

| 1. | 钱 | Qián | a Chinese surname |
| 2. | 蓝天大厦 | Lántiān Dàshà | the Blue Sky Tower |

注释 Zhùshì **Notes**

1 我想问一下，…… Excuse me, …

"我想问一下"，当你想问别人问题时，可以先用这句话来引起对方注意，然后提出要问的问题。

When you want to ask someone about something, you can begin with "我想问一下" to arouse the attention of the listener, and then ask your question.

2 你们想租多大面积的？ How large a room do you want?

"多 + 长 / 大 / 重 / 高"，用来询问长度、面积、年龄、重量和高度。例如：

In Chinese, people usually use "多 + 长 / 大 / 重 / 高" to ask about the length, area, age, weight or height. For example,

问长度	Ask about length	这条路多长？
问年龄	Ask about age	你今年多大？
问面积	Ask about area	你的房子多大（面积）？
问重量	Ask about weight	这个箱子多重？
问高度	Ask about height	他多高？

3 一平米一天多少钱？ What's the rent for one square meter per day?

主谓谓语句。我们在第八单元课文二中已经学过。小谓语有时候是数量短语，有时候是形容词短语。例如：

This is a subject-predicate predicate sentence. We have already learned this in Text 2 of Unit 8. The minor predicate can be a numeral-classifier compound, or an adjectival phrase. For example,

大主语 Major subject	大谓语 Major predicate	
	小主语 Minor subject	小谓语 Minor predicate
他	工作	很忙。（Adj）
这课	汉字	很多。（Adj）
一平米	一天	多少钱？（Q）
一个车位	一个月	多少钱？（Q）
200 平米	一个月	3 万左右。（Q）
地上车位	一个月	300 块。（Q）

4 有没有免租期？ Is there a rent-free period?

正反疑问句。我们在第三单元课文一中学过。这里是动词"有"的肯定形式和它的否定形式"没有"组成的正反疑问句。肯定的回答是"有"，否定的回答是"没有"。例如：

This is an affirmative-negative question. We have already learned about some affirmative-negative questions in Text 1 of Unit 3. This affirmative-negative question is of the verb "有" and its negative form "没有". The affirmative answer to it is "有", and the negative answer is "没有". For example,

问 Question	肯定回答 Positive Answer	否定回答 Negative Answer
明天你去不去天安门？	去。	不去。
你想不想吃中国菜？	想。	不想。
你买不买汉语书？	买。	不买。

本句中，"免租期"是"有"的宾语。在动词作谓语的正反疑问句中，动词后有宾语时，疑问形式有三种：（1）V 不 V + O，上面的例句都是这种形式；（2）V + O +不V，如"你买汉语书不买"；（3）V + O + 不 V + O，如"你买汉语书不买汉语书"，但是这种不常用。

"免租期" is the object of "有". When there is an object after the predicate verb in an affirmative-negative question, there are three interrogative forms: (1) "V 不 V + O", like all the examples given above; (2) "V + O + 不 V", e.g. "你买汉语书不买"; (3) "V + O + 不 V+ O", which is not often used, e.g. "你买汉语书不买汉语书".

5 您随时可以过来看房。**You can come to take a look at any time.**

"过来"，动词，表示从另一个地方到说话人所在的地方来。我们在第二单元课文二已经学过这个词。例如：

The verb "过来" means to come to the place where the speaker is. We have already learned this word in Text 2 of Unit 2. For example,

情境 Situation	例句 Sentence
经理对自己的秘书说：	王秘书，请过来一下。
北京的王先生对天津的朋友说：	北京有很多好玩儿的地方，你过来玩儿吧。
小张的朋友周末要来小张家，小张说：	你过来的时候先给我打个电话吧。

Kāng Àilì de Bàngōngshì
康爱丽的办公室
Alice's office

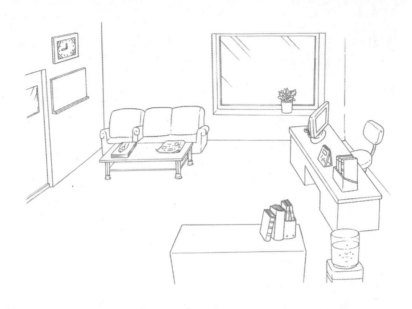

Kāng Àilì de bàngōngshì suīrán bú dà, dànshì hěn gānjìng. Fángjiān zhōngyāng
康爱丽的办公室虽然不大，但是很干净。房间中央
yǒu yì zhāng bàngōngzhuō hé yì bǎ zhuànyǐ, zhuōzi shang fàngzhe yì tái diànnǎo、
有一张办公桌和一把转椅，桌子上放着一台电脑、
yì běn táilì hé jǐ ge wénjiànjiā.
一本台历和几个文件夹。

Alice's office is not large but very clean. In the middle of the room, there is a desk
and a swivel chair, and on the desk there is a computer, a calendar and several folders.

Fángjiān de zuǒbian yǒu yí ge dà chuānghu, chuānghu cháo nán, guāngxiàn
房间的左边有一个大窗户，窗户朝南，光线
hěn hǎo, chuāngtái shang bǎizhe yì pén huā. Kào chuāng fàngzhe yì zǔ shāfā,
很好，窗台上摆着一盆花。靠窗放着一组沙发，
shāfā qiánmian yǒu yí ge chájī, chájī shang fàngzhe yí fèn bàozhǐ hé jǐ běn zázhì.
沙发前面有一个茶几，茶几上放着一份报纸和几本杂志。
Chuānghu duìmiàn kào qiáng fàngzhe yí ge shūguì, shūguì li yǒu yìxiē shū hé zīliào.
窗户对面靠墙放着一个书柜，书柜里有一些书和资料。

Shūguì pángbiān fàngzhe yì tái yǐnshuǐjī.

书柜旁边放着一台饮水机。

On the left of the room is a big window, facing south. The room is well-lighted. On the window sill there is a pot of flowers. Near the window there is a set of sofas with a tea table in front. On the tea table there is a newspaper and several magazines. Opposite to the window is a bookcase against the wall, where there are some books and materials in it. Beside the bookcase is a water dispenser.

Bàngōngzhuō duìmiàn de qiáng shang guàzhe yí ge zhōng，zhōng de xiàmian

办公桌对面的墙上挂着一个钟，钟的下面

yǒu yí kuài báibǎn.

有一块白板。

There is a clock hung on the wall opposite to the desk, and under the clock is a whiteboard.

生词 Shēngcí	**New Words**		
1. 办公室	bàngōngshì	N	office
2. 虽然	suīrán	Conj	though, although
3. 但是	dànshì	Conj	but
4. 房间	fángjiān	N	room
5. 中央	zhōngyāng	N	center
6. 张	zhāng	M	*a measure word*
7. 办公桌	bàngōngzhuō	N	desk, bureau
8. 把	bǎ	M	*a measure word*
9. 转椅	zhuànyǐ	N	swivel chair
10. 桌子	zhuōzi	N	desk, table
11. 放	fàng	V	to put
12. 着	zhe	AP	*indicating the continuation of a state*
13. 台	tái	M	*a measure word (for home appliances)*

14. 台历	táilì	N	desk calendar
15. 文件夹	wénjiànjiā	N	file folder
16. 左边	zuǒbian	N	left, left side
17. 窗户	chuānghu	N	window
18. 朝	cháo	V	to face
19. 光线	guāngxiàn	N	light
20. 窗台	chuāngtái	N	window sill
21. 摆	bǎi	V	to put
22. 盆	pén	N	pot, basin
23. 靠	kào	V	to lean against
24. 组	zǔ	M	*a measure word*
25. 前面	qiánmian	N	front
26. 茶几	chájī	N	tea table
27. 报纸	bàozhǐ	N	newspaper
28. 杂志	zázhì	N	magazine
29. 对面	duìmiàn	N	the opposite side
30. 墙	qiáng	N	wall
31. 书柜	shūguì	N	bookcase
32. 里	li	N	inside
33. 一些	yìxiē	Q	some
34. 资料	zīliào	N	material
35. 旁边	pángbiān	N	side
36. 饮水机	yǐnshuǐjī	N	water dispenser
37. 挂	guà	V	to hang
38. 钟	zhōng	N	clock
39. 下面	xiàmian	N	below, under
40. 块	kuài	M	*a measure word*
41. 白板	báibǎn	N	whiteboard

注释 Zhùshì **Notes**

1 康爱丽的办公室虽然不大，但是很干净。Alice's office is not large but very clean.

"虽然……，但是……"，转折复句。前一分句说明一种情况，后一分句不是顺着这种情况得出结论，而是给出另一种相反或者部分相反的情况。"虽然"可以放在前一个分句的主语前或后，"但是"必须放在后一个分句的最前面。有时候"虽然"可以省略，语气上显得缓和一些。例如：

In a transitional compound sentence, the former clause explains one situation, and the latter clause, instead of drawing a conclusion based on the situation, introduces an opposite or a partly opposite situation. "虽然……，但是……" is a transitional compound sentence often used. "虽然" can be put either before or after the subject of the former clause, but "但是" must be put at the very beginning of the latter clause. Sometimes "虽然" can be omitted, making the mood mild. For example,

虽然 + subject of clause 1 / subject of clause 1 + 虽然		但是 + clause 2
虽然我会游泳		游得不太好。
他虽然会说汉语，	但是	说得不太流利（liúlì, fluent）。
这个房间有空调，		不凉快。
王经理的办公室（虽然）很小，		很干净。

2 桌子上放着一台电脑。On the desk there is a computer.

"着"，动态助词，这里用于存在句中，描写处所或人的穿着打扮，这时的"着"具有描写作用。例如：

"着", an aspect particle, is used here in an existential sentence to indicate the state of some place or describe how someone is dressed. It is of the descriptive function. For example,

S（Place）	V（Verb）	AP（着）	O（Nu + M + N）
桌子上	放		一本书。
窗台上	摆		一盆花。
书柜里	放	着	一些资料。
墙上	挂		一个钟。
她	穿		一件 T 恤衫。

用"着"的存在句和我们在第六单元课文一中学过的动词为"有"的存在句一样，都可以表示什么地方有什么物或人，不过"动词 + 着"更强调物或人所处的状态、存在的方式。

例如:

Same as the existential sentence with the verb "有", which we have already learned in Text 1 of Unit 6, the existential sentence with "着" can indicate there is something or somebody somewhere, but it lays more stress on the state of the person or thing, or the way how the person or thing exists. For example,

PW+ 有 +O（Nu+M+N）	PW+V+ 着 +O（Nu+M+N）
茶几上有几本杂志。	茶几上放着几本杂志。
沙发前面有一个茶几。	沙发前面放着一个茶几。
办公桌对面的墙上有一个钟。	办公桌对面的墙上挂着一个钟。
窗台上有一盆花。	窗台上摆着一盆花。

练习 Liànxí · **Exercises**

一 跟读生词，注意发音和声调。
Read the new words after the teacher and pay attention to your pronunciation and tones.

二 跟读课文，注意语音语调。
Read the texts after the teacher and pay attention to your pronunciation and intonation.

三 学生分组，分角色朗读课文一、二；学生分段朗读课文三。
Divide the students into groups and read Texts 1 & 2 in different roles. Read Text 3 paragraph by paragraph.

四 学生分组，不看书，分角色表演课文一、二；不看书，介绍康爱丽的办公室。
Divide the students into groups and play the roles in Texts 1 & 2 without referring to the book. Talk about Alice's office without referring to the book.

五 角色扮演。（提示：角色可以互换。）
Role playing. (Note: the roles can be exchanged.)

1. 一个学生扮演房东 A，另一个学生扮演想租房子的人 B。B 向 A 询问房子的情况以及租金的问题。
   Student A acts as the landlord, and student B acts as the person who wants to rent the apartment. B asks A something about the apartment and the rent.

2. 一个学生扮演负责租售写字楼的经理 A，另一个学生 B 想租写字楼，B 给 A 打电话询问写字楼的情况和租金的问题。
   Student A acts as the manager who is in charge of the rental and sales department, and student B acts as the person who wants to rent an office. B calls A to ask about the office building and the rent.

3. 请介绍（可以根据自己的情况任选一个题目）：
   Choose a topic to talk about.

   （1）你的教室　　Your classroom

   （2）你知道的一间办公室　　An office you know

   （3）你理想的办公室　　Your ideal office

六 复述课文一和课文二。
Retell Texts 1 & 2.

七 把下面的动词和它的宾语用线连起来。
Connect the following verbs with their corresponding objects with lines.

贴　　　　　　　中介费

付　　　　　　　写字楼

租　　　　　　　广告

靠近　　　　　　合同

签　　　　　　　马路

八 填写正确的量词。
Fill in the blanks with right measure words.

一（　　）桌子　　　一（　　）转椅　　　一（　　）电脑

一（　　）台历　　　一（　　）文件夹　　　一（　　）花

一（　　）沙发　　　一（　　）茶几　　　一（　　）报纸

一（　　）杂志　　　一（　　）书柜　　　一（　　）书

一（　　）饮水机　　　一（　　）钟　　　一（　　）白板

九 选词填空。
Fill in the blanks with the given words.

| 商量 | 合适 | 随时 | 包括 | 方便 | 最好 |
| 麻烦 | 着急 | 慢慢 | 起来 | 另外 | |

① 他已经找了一个月房子了，还没有找到（　　）的。

② 卧室（　　）有阳台。

③ 别（　　），这样的房子很多，（　　）找，一定能找到的。

④ 我觉得找中介公司更（　　），还是自己找吧。

⑤ 我想（　　）了，学校西门往北100米有一家银行。

⑥ 那个小区附近有超市、邮局和菜市场，非常（　　）。

⑦ 请问，你的房租（　　）物业费吗？

⑧ 我每天得学习8个小时汉语，（　　），晚上还要工作两个小时。

⑨ 这件事我得跟我爱人（àiren，husband or wife）（　　）一下。

⑩ 您（　　）可以过来参观。

✚ 替换练习。
Substitution drills.

① <u>这些房子</u> 有的 <u>离学校太远</u>，有的 <u>靠近马路</u>，还有的呢，<u>房租太高了</u>。

这些书	是英文的	是中文的	是法文的
同学们	在看书	在聊天儿	在上网
我们周末	去长城	去故宫	在家休息
这些广告	是出租房子的	是求租的	是卖房的

② <u>我的一个朋友</u> 让 <u>中介公司</u> 帮 <u>她</u> <u>租了</u> <u>一套房子</u>。

卡尔	王老师	他	找了	一个辅导老师
康爱丽	卡尔	她	买	一本书
卡尔	李明明	他	买	一瓶水
王经理	秘书	他	预订	一张机票

③ <u>找中介公司</u> <u>省事</u> 倒是 挺 <u>省事</u> 的，可是 <u>她得付中介费</u>。

房子	大	大	不太干净
衣服	漂亮	漂亮	太贵了
菜	好吃	好吃	太辣了
交通	方便	方便	人很多

④ 一平米　一天　多少钱?

一平米	一天	5 块钱
100 平米	一个月	3 万
地上车位	一个月	600 块
路边的车位	一个小时	2 块钱
这种房间	一天	200 块

⑤ 如果　您签了合同,我们　就　可以给您20天的装修时间。

明天不下雨	我们	去长城
你下午有时间	我们	去看电影
你买三件	我	给你便宜 10 块钱
附近有地铁站	卡尔	租那个小区的房子

⑥ 康爱丽的办公室　虽然　不大,但是　很干净。

那个饭馆的菜	很好吃	很贵
今天的天气	很暖和	有点儿风
房租	很便宜	面积很小
他	会做中国菜	做得不好吃

⑦ 桌子上　放　着　一台电脑。

墙上	挂	一个钟
茶几上	放	一份报纸
靠窗	放	一组沙发
窗台上	摆	一盆花

十一 用下面的词语组成句子。
Make sentences with the following words and expressions.

① 一直　听说　你　房子　在　找

② 什么样　你　租　房子　打算　的

③ 一点儿　客厅　大　最好

④ 阳台　更好了　卧室　那就　如果　有

⑤ 在楼道里　有人　贴　楼上　广告　了

⑥ 小区　那个　附近　在　就　学校　咱们

⑦ 就　那　你　拜托　了

⑧ 写字楼　大厦　有　出租　吗　你们　还

⑨ 和　物业费　包括　吗　停车费

⑩ 老板　得　一下　我　商量　跟

⑪ 您　过来　看房　随时　可以

⑫ 窗户　一个　靠墙　对面　书柜　放着

十二 完成下面的兼语句。
Complete the following pivotal sentences.

Example：我的一个朋友让中介公司帮她租了一套房子。（"中介公司"是兼语）

① 卡尔让康爱丽＿＿＿＿＿＿＿＿＿＿＿＿＿＿＿＿＿＿。

② 康爱丽请王老师＿＿＿＿＿＿＿＿＿＿＿＿＿＿＿＿＿。

③ 王经理叫秘书_____。

④ 我们小区有人_____。

⑤ 卡尔请客户_____。

⑥ 我们学校有学生_____。

十三 对画线部分进行提问。
Ask a question about the underlined part.

Example：他哥哥<u>两米</u>。——→ 他哥哥多高？

① 他 <u>1.7 米</u>。——→

② 这个办公室 <u>100 平米</u>。——→

③ 小王 <u>32 岁</u>。——→

④ 这件行李 <u>10 公斤</u>。——→

⑤ 从家到学校 <u>1 公里</u>（gōnglǐ，kilometer）。——→

⑥ 这条裤子 <u>3 尺</u>（chǐ，traditional Chinese unit of length）长。——→

十四 把下面的句子改为正反疑问句，并给出肯定和否定两种回答。
Rewrite the following sentences into affirmative-negative questions, and give both affirmative and negative answers.

Example：你去天安门吗？——→你去不去天安门？ 去。/ 不去。

① 你们班有法国人吗？——→

② 你有女朋友吗？——→

③ 你想去上海玩儿吗？——→

④ 你喜欢吃饺子吗？——→

十五 用所给词语完成对话。

Complete the dialogues with the given words or expressions.

① A：你这几天忙什么呢？

B：_____。（一直）

② A：我要去天津出差，怎么去呢？

B：_____。（最好)

③ A：你明天去不去长城？

B：_____。（如果……，就……）

④ A：课间休息的时候，同学们都在做什么？

B：_____。

（有的……，有的……，还有的……）

⑤ A：你们小区的交通很方便吧？

B：_____。

（……倒是……，可是……）

⑥ A：你家附近有地铁吗？

B：_____。（……倒是……，就是……）

⑦ A：你觉得那家饭馆的菜怎么样？

B：_____。（有点儿）

⑧ A：你们学校旁边的那个写字楼怎么样？

B：_____。（虽然……，但是……）

十六 用给出的词语和"着"造存在句。

Make up existential sentences with the given words and "着".

词语 Words		基本结构 The basic structure：PW＋V＋着＋O（Nu＋M＋N）
桌子	电脑	桌子上放着一台电脑。
茶几	书	
书柜	资料	
房间	沙发	
墙	画儿	
卧室	床	

（续表）

词语 Words		基本结构 The basic structure：PW＋V＋着＋O（Nu＋M＋N）
白板	饮水机	
办公桌	台历	
文件夹	合同	

十七 阅读理解。
Reading comprehension.

　　最近，卡尔在经贸大学附近租了一套两居室的房子，他对这套房子非常满意。厨房和卫生间都有窗户，客厅很大，卧室都朝南，光线非常好。房子里的电器都是新的，房租也不太贵。小区里有很多树和草地，很安静。附近有一个很大的超市，卡尔常常去那里买东西。小区的南边还有一个公园，周末的时候，卡尔就去那里散散步、看看书。能租到这样的房子，卡尔觉得自己很幸运。

生词　Shēngcí　**New Words**

1. 满意	mǎnyì	V	to be satisfied
2. 树	shù	N	tree
3. 草地	cǎodì	N	grassland
4. 安静	ānjìng	Adj	quiet
5. 散步	sàn bù	V//O	to take a walk

判断正误：

Decide if the following statements are true or false:

（　　）❶ 房子的厨房和卫生间都很大。

（　　）❷ 房子的客厅朝南。

（　　）❸ 卡尔觉得他租的房子非常好。

（　　）❹ 卡尔租的房子可能靠近马路。

（　　）⑤卡尔购物非常方便。

（　　）⑥卡尔每天都去公园散步。

 完成任务：请用课文中学过的词语和句子完成任务。
Complete the tasks: Please complete the tasks with the words and sentences you have learned in the texts.

---

1. 你的朋友想租一套公寓，请帮他写一个求租广告。
One of your friends wants to rent an apartment. Help him to write an apartment wanted ad.

2. 请你打电话或亲自去咨询一下你想知道的写字楼的出租情况，并把相关情况记下来，然后到课堂上向老师和同学报告。
Make a telephone call or go to an office building to get the information about renting an office you want to know and write it down, and then present the information you get to your teacher and classmates.

我要开一个储蓄账户
I want to open a savings account

课文 Text	题目 Title	注释 Notes
一	您要办什么业务 Can I help you	1．"（是）……，还是……" 2．"比"字句（复习） The "比" sentence (Review) 3．无主语兼语句 The pivotal sentence without a subject 4．副词"经常" The adverb "经常" 5．多项状语的顺序 The sequence of multiple adverbial modifiers 6．副词"顺便" The adverb "顺便"
二	我来银行取点儿钱 I come to the bank to withdraw some money	1．"没想到" 2．形容词"巧" The adjective "巧" 3．"不 A 也不 B" 4．动词"爆" The verb "爆" 5．叹词"哦" The interjection "哦" 6．副词"原来" The adverb "原来" 7．"原来是这样" 8．指示代词"这么" The demonstrative pronoun "这么" 9．副词"好像" The adverb "好像"
三	分期付款 Payment by installment	1．"很"＋"有"／表示心理感知的动词 "很"＋"有"／The verb denoting mental perception 2．程度副词"比较" The degree adverb "比较"

Nín Yào Bàn Shénme Yèwù

您要办什么业务

Can I help you

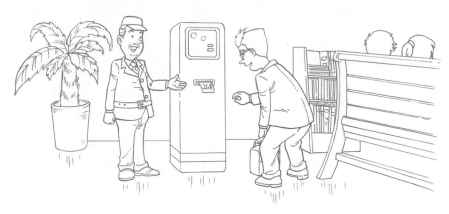

Kǎ'ěr láidào yì jiā yínháng.

卡尔来到一家银行。

Karl comes to a bank.

Kǎ'ěr: Qǐngwèn, zài nǎr páiduì?

● 卡尔: 请问，在哪儿排队？

Karl: Excuse me, where should I queue?

Bǎo'ān: Búyòng páiduì. Xiānsheng, qǐng nín xiān ná hào, ránhòu zuò zài

○ 保安: 不用排队。先生，请您先拿号，然后坐在

nàbiān děng jiù kěyǐ le.

那边等就可以了。

Safeguard: You don't have to queue, sir. You can take a number and then sit there

waiting.

Kǎ'ěr nádào de shì èrbǎi liùshíbā hào, děngle yíhuìr, dào tā le.

卡尔拿到的是268号，等了一会儿，到他了。

The number Karl takes is No. 268. After waiting for a while, it is his turn.

Guǎngbō: Qǐng èrbǎi liùshíbā hào gùkè dào èr hào chuāngkǒu.

● 广播: 请 268 号顾客到 2 号窗口。

Announcement: No. 268, please come to window No. 2.

Yínháng zhíyuán: Nín hǎo! Qǐngwèn nín yào bàn shénme yèwù?

○ 银行职员: 您好！请问您要办什么业务？

Bank teller: Good morning! Can I help you?

Kǎ'ěr: Nín hǎo! Wǒ yào kāi yí ge chǔxù zhànghù.

● 卡尔: 您好！我要开一个储蓄账户。

Karl: Good morning! I want to open a savings account.

Yínháng zhíyuán: Huóqī háishi dìngqī?

○ 银行职员: 活期还是定期？

Bank teller: Current deposit or fixed deposit?

Kǎ'ěr: Yǒu shénme bù tóng ma?

● 卡尔: 有什么不同吗？

Karl: Any difference?

Yínháng zhíyuán: Dìngqī cúnkuǎn de lìlù bǐ huóqī de gāo yìxiē.

○ 银行职员: 定期存款的利率比活期的高一些。

Bank teller: The interest rate of the fixed deposit account is a bit higher than that of the current one.

Kǎ'ěr: Háishi huóqī ba, yǒu rén jīngcháng gěi wǒ huìkuǎn, wǒ yě kěyǐ

● 卡尔: 还是活期吧，有人经常给我汇款，我也可以

suíshí qǔ kuǎn.

随时取款。

Karl: A current one please. I often receive remittances and it's convenient to withdraw the money at any time.

Yínháng zhíyuán: Nà jiànyì nín kāi kǎ ba. Chúle cún qián qǔ qián, hái kěyǐ xiāofèi,

○ 银行职员: 那建议您开卡吧。除了存钱取钱，还可以消费，

bǐ cúnzhé fāngbiàn.

比存折方便。

Bank teller: I suggest that you get a card. Besides depositing and withdrawing money, you can also use it for payment. It is more convenient than a deposit book.

Kǎ'ěr: Nà jiù bàn zhāng kǎ ba.
卡尔： 那就办张卡吧。
Karl: Then I will apply for a card.

Yínháng zhíyuán: Qǐng nín xiān tián yíxià zhè zhāng biǎo. Nín dài hùzhào le ma?
银行职员： 请您先填一下这张表。您带护照了吗？
Bank teller: Please fill in this form first. Do you have your passport with you?

Kǎ'ěr: Dài le. Gěi nín.
卡尔： 带了。给您。
Karl: Yes, here you are.

Biǎo tiánwán le.
表填完了。
After the form is filled out.

Yínháng zhíyuán: Qǐng nín zài zhèr qiānzì.
银行职员： 请您在这儿签字。
Bank teller: Please sign your name here.

Kǎ'ěr: Zài nǎr qiān?
卡尔： 在哪儿签？
Karl: Where?

Yínháng zhíyuán: Xiàmian, "kèhù qiānzì".
银行职员： 下面，"客户签字"。
Bank teller: Right below here. See "Client's Signature".

Kǎ bànhǎo le.
卡办好了。
The card is ready.

Kǎ'ěr: Wǒ cún yíwàn. Shùnbiàn wèn yíxià, kěyǐ zài zìdòng qǔkuǎnjī
卡尔： 我存一万。顺便问一下，可以在自动取款机
shang zhuǎnzhàng ma?
上转账吗？
Karl: I'll deposit 10,000 *yuan*. By the way, can I make a transfer on an
ATM?

Yínháng zhíyuán: Dāngrán kěyǐ.
○ 银行职员： 当然可以。
Bank teller: Sure, you can.

Kǎ'ěr: Duì le, xiànzài ōuyuán duì rénmínbì de huìlǜ shì duōshao?
● 卡尔： 对了，现在欧元兑人民币的汇率是多少？
Karl: What's the exchange rate of EUR against RMB at present?

Yínháng zhíyuán: Bā diǎn bā sān ba. Nín kàn yíxià jīntiān de wàihuì páijiàbiǎo.
○ 银行职员： 8.83吧。您看一下今天的外汇牌价表。
Bank teller: 8.83. You can have a look at the List of Exchange Rate Quotation today.

Kǎ'ěr: Xièxie!
● 卡尔： 谢谢！
Karl: Thank you!

Yínháng zhíyuán: Nín yào huànqián ma?
○ 银行职员： 您要换钱吗？
Bank teller: Do you want to exchange money?

Kǎ'ěr: Jīntiān bú huàn. Zàijiàn!
● 卡尔： 今天不换。再见！
Karl: Not today. Goodbye!

Yínháng zhíyuán: Zàijiàn!
○ 银行职员： 再见！
Bank teller: Goodbye!

生词 Shēngcí **New Words**

1.	办	bàn	V	to do, to handle
2.	业务	yèwù	N	business
3.	排队	pái duì	V//O	to line up, to queue
4.	保安	bǎo'ān	N	safeguard
5.	拿	ná	V	to take
6.	广播	guǎngbō	N	announcement
7.	顾客	gùkè	N	customer

8.	窗口	chuāngkǒu	N	window
9.	银行	yínháng	N	bank
10.	职员	zhíyuán	N	office worker, staff member
11.	开	kāi	V	to open
12.	储蓄	chǔxù	V	to deposit
13.	账户	zhànghù	N	account
14.	活期	huóqī	Adj	current (deposit)
15.	定期	dìngqī	Adj	fixed (deposit)
16.	同	tóng	Adj	same, similar, equal
17.	存款	cúnkuǎn	N	deposit, savings deposit
18.	利率	lìlǜ	N	interest rate
19.	经常	jīngcháng	Adv	often
20.	汇款	huì kuǎn	V//O	to remit money
21.	取款	qǔ kuǎn		to withdraw money
22.	建议	jiànyì	V/N	to suggest; suggestion
23.	卡	kǎ	N	card
24.	存	cún	V	to deposit
25.	取	qǔ	V	to withdraw
26.	消费	xiāofèi	V	to consume
27.	存折	cúnzhé	N	deposit book
28.	填	tián	V	to fill in
29.	表	biǎo	N	form
30.	带	dài	V	to carry, to take, to bring
31.	护照	hùzhào	N	passport
32.	签字	qiān zì	V//O	to sign (one's name)
33.	顺便	shùnbiàn	Adv	by the way
34.	自动取款机	zìdòng qǔkuǎnjī		ATM
	自动	zìdòng	Adj	automatic

机	jī	N	machine
35. 转账	zhuǎn zhàng	V//O	to transfer accounts
36. 欧元	ōuyuán	N	Euro
37. 兑	duì	V	to exchange
38. 人民币	rénmínbì	N	RMB
39. 汇率	huìlǜ	N	exchange rate
40. 外汇牌价表	wàihuì páijiàbiǎo		List of Exchange Rate Quotation
外汇	wàihuì	N	foreign exchange
牌价	páijià	N	quotation
41. 换钱	huàn qián	V//O	to exchange money

注释 Zhùshì Notes

1 活期还是定期？ Current deposit or fixed deposit?

"（是）……还是……"，用于选择。回答时选择其中一项。句末可以带语气助词"呢、啊"，但是不能带"吗"。放在第一项之前的"是"可以省略。例如：

"（是）……还是……" is used for making a choice. The answer can be either A or B. The mood auxiliary "呢" or "啊" can be added at the end of the sentence, but "吗" cannot. The "是" before A can be omitted. For example,

① （是）你去，还是他去呢？

② 你（是）喜欢还是不喜欢？

③ （是）买灰的，还是买黑的？

口语中，常常就在要问的两项之间加上"还是"，省略其他成分。例如：

In oral Chinese, "还是" is usually added between the two alternatives, and other elements are omitted. For example,

④ 谁去开会？卡尔还是康爱丽？

⑤ 什么时候上课？上午还是下午？

⑥ 咖啡还是茶？

2 **定期存款的利率比活期的高一些。**

The interest rate of the fixed deposit account is a bit higher than that of the current one.

"比"字句。"比"字句用来比较两个事物性质、特点、具体数量或程度等的差别，基本结构："A 比 B + Adj+ 一些/多了/得多"。我们在第九单元课文二中学过。形容词后面用"一些"表示差别不大，用"多了、得多"表示差别大。例如：

The "比" sentence is used to show the difference in property, characteristic, amount or degree between two things. The basic structure is "A 比 B + adjective + 一些/多了/得多", which we have learned in Text 2 of Unit 9. "一些" is added after the adjective to show a minor difference, and "多了" or "得多" is added to show a large difference. For example,

陈述　Statement	比较　Comparison
昨天 28℃，今天 30℃。	今天比昨天热一些。
前天 10℃，昨天 28℃。	昨天的气温比前天高得多。
哥哥身高 180 cm，弟弟身高 182 cm。	弟弟比哥哥高一些。
妹妹身高 150 cm，姐姐身高 170 cm。	姐姐比妹妹高得多。
这件衣服 1000 块，那件衣服 1010 块。	那件衣服比这件衣服贵一些。
这件衣服 1000 块，那件衣服 3000 块。	那件衣服比这件衣服贵得多。

3 **有人经常给我汇款。** I often receive remittances.

无主语兼语句。谓语动词"有"的前面没有主语，兼语的谓语说明或描写兼语。"有"后面的宾语可以带"一些、很多、多少、（一）个、几个"等不定指的定语，表示新信息，不能用表示定指的"这个、那个"作定语。例如：

This is a pivotal sentence without a subject, in which there is no subject before the verb "有". The predicate of the pivot plays the role of explaining or describing the pivot. The object of "有" can take a non-referential attribute, such as "一些", "很多", "多少", "（一）个" or "几个", to provide some new information. The referential attributes, such as "这个" and "那个", cannot be used. For example,

① 有几个人不喜欢他。（√）

② 有一些学生去上海了。（√）

③ 有这个人给我汇款。（×）

④ 有那个人给我打电话。（×）

4 **有人经常给我汇款。** I often receive remittances.

"经常"，副词，意思是"常常"。表示事情的发生不止一次，而且时间相隔不久，在谓语动词前作状语。

"经常", an adverb, means "often". It indicates that something happens again and again during a short period of time. It is put before the predicate verb as an adverbial modifier.

5 有人经常给我汇款。 **I often receive remittances.**

多项状语的顺序。在汉语中，一个句子中有两个或两个以上的状语是多项状语。在本句中，兼语"人"的谓语是"汇款"，它的前面有两个状语：副词"经常"和由介词"给"组成的介词短语"给我"。一般多项状语的出现顺序是：（1）副词或副词短语；（2）形容词短语；（3）介词短语。例如：

The sequence of multiple adverbial modifiers should be noted. In Chinese, if there are two or more adverbial modifiers in a sentence, we call it a sentence with multiple adverbial modifiers. In the above sentence, the second predicate of the pivotal sentence is "汇款", before which there are two adverbial modifiers appearing in sequence, i.e. the adverb "经常" and the prepositional phrase "给我". The sequence of the multiple adverbial modifiers is: (1) adverb or adverbial phrase; (2) adjectival phrase; (3) prepositional phrase. For example,

S	P			
	Adv or adverbial phrase	Adjectival phrase	PP	VP
卡尔	经常		给妈妈	打电话。
他	已经		在北京	学过一个月汉语了。
王老师	每次都	耐心（nàixīn, patient）地	给我们	解答（jiědá, to answer）问题。

6 顺便问一下，…… **By the way, ...**

"顺便"，副词，表示乘着做某事的方便做另外一件事。"顺便问一下"，用来提出一个相关的问题希望对方解答，可以放在句首，也可以放在句中。例如：

"顺便", an adverb, indicates doing something by taking the advantage of doing something else. This sentence is used to raise a relevant question to the listener for an answer. It can be put either at the beginning or in the middle of a sentence. For example,

① 顺便问一下，到家乐福怎么走？
② 顺便问一下，银行几点下班？
③ 你去办公室的时候，顺便问一下怎么办饭卡。

Wǒ Lái Yínháng Qǔ Diǎnr Qián

我来银行取点儿钱

I come to the bank to withdraw some money

Zài xuéxiào pángbiān de yì jiā yínháng, Kǎ'ěr yùjianle
Lǐ Míngming.

在学校旁边的一家银行，卡尔遇见了李明明。

In a bank near the school, Karl runs into Li Mingming.

Lǐ Míngming: Hēi, Kǎ'ěr, méi xiǎngdào zài zhèr yùjian nǐ!

● 李明明： 嘿，卡尔，没想到在这儿遇见你！

Li Mingming: Hi, Karl. Fancy meeting you here.

Kǎ'ěr: Shì a, zhēn qiǎo! Wǒ lái yínháng qǔ diǎnr qián. Nǐ ne?

○ 卡尔： 是啊，真巧！我来银行取点儿钱。你呢？

Karl: What a coincidence! I come to the bank to withdraw some money. What
about you?

Lǐ Míngming: Wǒ bù qǔ qián yě bù cún qián, wǒ huán qián lái le.

● 李明明： 我不取钱也不存钱，我还钱来了。

Li Mingming: Neither withdrawing money nor depositing it, I come to pay back the
money.

78

Kǎ'ěr: Huán qián?

○ 卡尔： 还钱？

Karl: Pay back?

Lǐ Míngming: Duì a, wǒ de xìnyòngkǎ dōu shuābào le, děi gǎnjǐn huán qián.

● 李明明： 对啊，我的信用卡都刷爆了，得赶紧还钱。

Li Mingming: Right. I must pay back now, for my credit card is maxed out.

Kǎ'ěr: Ò, yuánlái shì zhèyàng. Yínháng li zěnme zhème duō rén?

○ 卡尔： 哦，原来是这样。银行里怎么这么多人？

Karl: Oh, I see. Why are there so many people in the bank?

Lǐ Míngming: Xiànzài shuǐfèi、diànfèi、wǎngfèi、diànhuàfèi、ránqìfèi děng, dōu

● 李明明： 现在水费、电费、网费、电话费、燃气费等，都

kěyǐ zài yínháng jiāo, rén dāngrán jiù duō le.

可以在银行交，人当然就多了。

Li Mingming: All kinds of fees, like charges for water, electricity, Internet, telephone, and gas, can be paid in the bank nowadays. That's why there are so many people here.

Kǎ'ěr: Hǎoxiàng hái yǒu hěn duō rén zài mǎi jījīn.

○ 卡尔： 好像还有很多人在买基金。

Karl: It seems that there are also many people buying funds here.

生词 Shēngcí **New Words**

1. 没想到	méi xiǎngdào		unexpectedly
2. 遇见	yùjian	V	to meet
3. 巧	qiǎo	Adj	coincidental
4. 还	huán	V	to pay back
5. 信用卡	xìnyòngkǎ	N	credit card
6. 刷	shuā	V	to swipe, to punch (a card)
7. 爆	bào	V	to explode
8. 赶紧	gǎnjǐn	Adv	at once

9. 哦	ò	Int	*used to express realization and understanding*
10. 原来	yuánlái	Adv	originally
11. 燃气	ránqì	N	gas
12. 等	děng	Pt	and so on, etc.
13. 交	jiāo	V	to pay
14. 好像	hǎoxiàng	Adv	as if
15. 基金	jījīn	N	fund

注释　Zhùshì　**Notes**

1 没想到在这儿遇见你！ **Fancy meeting you here.**

　　"没想到"，指出现的情况或发生的事情出乎意料，必须是已经发生的情况或事情。"没想到"后面常常是一个句子。例如：

　　"没想到" indicates what happened goes beyond the speaker's expectation. "没想到" is often followed by a sentence. For example,

	北京的天气这么冷！
没想到	卡尔送给我一个大蛋糕。
	她有两个孩子。

2 真巧！我来银行取点儿钱。**What a coincidence! I come to the bank to withdraw some money.**

　　"巧"，形容词，表示恰好，正遇上某种机会。可以作谓语。口语中常说"真巧"、"真不巧"，常用在句子的开头，有时用在动词"来"的后面作补语。例如：

　　"巧", an adjective, means "coincidental" and can serve as the predicate. In spoken Chinese, "真巧" and "真不巧" are often used at the beginning of sentences. Sometimes, they can be put after the verb

"来" as the complement. For example,

① 真巧，我一出门就碰到他了。

② 真巧，我正要去找你，你就来了。

③ 她来得真巧。

④ 真不巧，他现在不在办公室。

⑤ 真不巧，下雨了，不能去长城了。

⑥ 她来得真不巧。

3 **我不取钱也不存钱。Neither withdrawing money nor depositing it.**

"不 A 也不 B"，A、B 为同类的动词、动词短语或形容词，两个词语并列，表示主语同时不具有两方面的行为、性质或情况。例如：

In the structure "不 A 也不 B", A and B are verbs, verbal phrases or adjectives of the same kind, indicating that the subject does not possess either of the actions, properties or situations. For example,

① 他不吃也不喝。

② 我不吸烟也不喝酒。

③ 我的朋友不漂亮也不温柔（wēnróu, tender）。

4 **我的信用卡都刷爆了。My credit card is maxed out.**

"爆"，动词，用在其他动词的后面表示该动作的结果，口语中常用"动词 + 爆"表示数量增加得很快，突破了一定的限制。例如：

"爆", a verb, is put after another verb to show the result of an action. In spoken Chinese, "V + 爆" is often used to indicate that the quantity increases fast and has broken through a certain limit. For example,

S	P	
	V	V（爆）+MdPt（了）
信用卡	刷	爆了。
电话	打	
邮箱	发	

5 **哦，原来是这样。 Oh, I see.**

"哦"，叹词，表示领会、醒悟。例如：

"哦", an exclamation, indicates that the speaker understands something. For example,

① 哦，我知道了。

② 哦，我懂了。

6 **哦，原来是这样。Oh, I see.**

"原来"，副词，表示发现真实的情况。可以放在动词、形容词前，作状语。也可以放在句首。例如：

"原来", an adverb, indicates that the speaker gets to know a true situation. It can be put before a verb or an adjective as the adverbial modifier and can also be put at the beginning of a sentence. For example,

① 房间这么热，原来是空调坏了。
② 原来你这么喜欢吃巧克力。
③ 原来是你呀！

7 **哦，原来是这样。Oh, I see.**

"原来是这样"，表示发现了从前不知道的情况，明白了原因，含有"醒悟"的意思。也可以说"原来如此"。"这样"，指示代词，指示情况、状态。例如：

"原来是这样" indicates that the speaker gets to know the situation or reason that he/she didn't know before. "原来如此" can also be used. "这样", a demonstrative pronoun, indicates situation or state. For example,

A: 卡尔今天为什么没来上班？
B: 他病了。
A: 哦，原来是这样。

8 **银行里怎么这么多人？Why are there so many people in the bank?**

"这么"，指示代词，表示程度，作状语，后面可以带形容词、表示心理活动的动词（如"想、喜欢"等）、有使令意义的动词（如"叫、让"等）和能愿动词。基本结构："这么 + Adj / VP"。这一结构加上"的"可以作定语。例如：

"这么", a demonstrative pronoun, indicates degree. It usually serves as the adverbial modifier in a sentence and can be followed by an adjective, a verb denoting mental activity (such as"想", "喜欢", etc.), a causative verb (such as"叫", "让", etc.), or an optative verb. The commonly used structure is "这么 + Adj / VP", which can serve as the attribute if "的" is added. For example,

① 你怎么这么喜欢喝咖啡？
② 没想到你这么会说话。
③ 这么热的天气！

9 **好像还有很多人在买基金。It seems that there are also many people buying funds here.**

"好像"，副词，"似乎、大概"的意思，表示不确定的推测、判断或感觉。有时用在主语前，有时用在主语后。例如：

"好像", an adverb, means "as if", similar to "似乎" and "大概". It indicates an uncertain speculation, judgement or feeling. It can be put either before or after the subject. For example,

① 明天好像会下雨。

② 她好像有点儿不舒服。

③ 好像有很多人在交电话费。

Fēnqī Fù Kuǎn
分期付款
Payment by installment

Lǐ Míngming zuìjìn mǎile yì tái bǐjìběn diànnǎo, shì yòng xìnyòngkǎ fēnqī
李明明最近买了一台笔记本电脑，是用信用卡分期
fù kuǎn de. Suīrán "líng shǒufù、líng lìxī" de fù kuǎn fāngshì hěn yǒu yòuhuòlì,
付款的。虽然"零首付、零利息"的付款方式很有诱惑力，
dànshì shǒuxùfèi bǐjiào gāo. Zuìhòu, Lǐ Míngming háishi xuǎnzéle shǒufù
但是手续费比较高。最后，李明明还是选择了首付
bǎi fēnzhī èrshí, liánxù gōng yì nián de fù kuǎn fāngshì. Tā juéde zhè zhǒng fù kuǎn
20%，连续供一年的付款方式。她觉得这种付款
fāngshì bǐjiào shìhé zìjǐ, yě bǐjiào huásuàn.
方式比较适合自己，也比较划算。

Li Mingming bought a laptop recently by installment via the credit card. Although the paying method of "zero down payment, zero interest rate" is very attractive, the handling charge is too high. At last, Li Mingming chose the method of making a 20% down payment and paying monthly for a year, which she thinks is more suitable for her and more economical.

生词 Shēngcí **New Words**

1. 分期	fēnqī	V	by installment
2. 付款	fù kuǎn		to pay
3. 笔记本电脑	bǐjìběn diànnǎo		laptop
4. 首付	shǒufù	N	down payment
5. 方式	fāngshì	N	method, way
6. 诱惑力	yòuhuòlì	N	attractiveness
7. 手续	shǒuxù	N	procedure
8. 最后	zuìhòu	N	end, at last
9. 选择	xuǎnzé	V	to choose
10. 连续	liánxù	V	continuously
11. 供	gōng	V	to supply
12. 种	zhǒng	M	a kind, a sort, a type
13. 适合	shìhé	V	to suit, to fit
14. 划算	huásuàn	Adj	economical

注释 Zhùshì **Notes**

1 虽然"零首付、零利息"的付款方式很有诱惑力，……

Although the paying method of "zero down payment, zero interest rate" is very attractive, ...

"很" + "有" / 表示心理感知的动词。程度副词"很"可以放在形容词前面，也可以放在一些表示心理感知的动词和某些动宾短语的前面。例如：

The degree adverb "很" can be put before adjectives, verbs denoting mental perception, or some verb-object phrases. For example,

很	喜欢、想、爱、希望、愿意	表示心理感知的动词 Verbs denoting mental perception
	有道理、有钱、有办法、有头脑、有经验	动宾短语 Verb-object phrases

2 她觉得这种付款方式比较适合自己，也比较划算。

She thinks this paying method is more suitable for her and more economical.

"比较"，程度副词，表示有一定的、不太高的程度。我们在第九单元课文二中已经学过。需要注意的是，"比较"常常不用于比较，后边一般也不能用否定副词，如不说"她比较不好"、"今天比较不热"等。

"比较", a degree adverb, indicates a certain degree, which is not very high, and we have learned it in Text 2 of Unit 9. More often it does not involve comparison and cannot be followed by negative adverbs. For example, we don't say "她比较不好" or "今天比较不热".

练习 Liànxí **Exercises**

一 跟读生词，注意发音和声调。
Read the new words after the teacher and pay attention to your pronunciation and tones.

二 跟读课文，注意语音语调。
Read the texts after the teacher and pay attention to your pronunciation and intonation.

三 学生分组，分角色朗读课文一、二。
Divide the students into groups and read Texts 1 & 2 in different roles.

四 学生分组，不看书，分角色表演课文一、二。
Divide the students into groups and play the roles in Texts 1 & 2 without referring to the book.

五 角色扮演。（提示：角色可以互换。）
Role playing. (Note: the roles can be exchanged.)

1. 假设 A 和 B 两个人在银行里相遇，用课文里学过的词语和句子完成一段对话。
   Two students A and B come across each other in the bank and have a talk. Make a dialogue with the words and sentences that have been learned from the texts.

2. A 和 B 来自两个不同的国家（或是同一个国家），互相问答：
   Two students A and B coming from different countries (or the same country) have a talk.

   (1) 在自己国家买东西可以采用什么样的付款方式；
   Talk about the paying methods in their own countries.

   (2) 询问对方喜欢什么样的付款方式以及为什么。
   Ask what is the other party's favorite paying method and why.

六 朗读课文三并复述。
Read and retell Text 3.

七 替换练习。
Substitution drills.

① 请问，在哪儿 排队？

买票

换钱

办卡

交费

注册（zhùcè, to register）

② 请 268 号顾客 到 2号窗口。

请	你的朋友	来	北京玩儿
叫	卡尔	去	办公室
让	张远	点	菜
派	康爱丽	去	上海

③ 有 人 经常给我汇款。

客人	来了
一个学生	没来
一些人	知道这件事
很多人	办信用卡

④ 不 取钱 也不 存钱。

好	坏
胖	瘦
冷	热
吃	喝
想唱歌	想跳舞
打算回国	打算去旅行

⑤ <u>银行里</u> 怎么这么 多 <u>人</u>?

上海	雨
你	书
电话费	钱
菜里	辣椒（làjiāo, chilli）

⑥ 好像 <u>还有很多人在买基金</u>。

> 他不太高兴
>
> 小王有女朋友了
>
> 天要下雨了
>
> 你昨晚没睡好

⑦ <u>李明明的电脑</u> 是 <u>用信用卡分期付款</u> 的。

卡尔	6月来北京
他们	在北京认识
我	坐飞机去上海
小王	去机场接我

八 用下面的词语组成句子。
Make sentences with the following words and expressions.

① 储蓄　要　一个　我　账户　开

② 活期的　比　利率　高　一些　定期存款的

③ 取款　可以　也　随时　我

④ 这张表　请　先　您　一下　填

⑤ 您　在　请　签字　这儿

⑥ 欧元　汇率　人民币　多少　的　是　兑

⑦ 在　遇见　这儿　没想到　你

⑧ 我　取　来　点儿　银行　钱

⑨ 都　我　信用卡　的　刷爆了

九 完成下面的句子或对话。
Complete the following sentences or dialogues.

① 这件衣服太贵了，还是_____。

② 我的汉语不太好，还是_____。

③ A：我们吃中国菜还是吃日本菜？

　　B：_____，还是_____。

④ A：周末我们骑自行车去长城吧？

　　B：_____，还是_____。

⑤ 您好，我办一张信用卡。顺便问一下，_____？

⑥ 请问，超市怎么走？顺便问一下，附近有_____？

⑦ 下课你去小卖部（xiǎomàibù, grocery）的时候，顺便_____。

⑧ 我回国的时候，顺便_____。

⑨ 我好像见过你，对了，_____？

⑩ 对了，我忘了告诉你，_____？

⑪ 我第一次见她，没想到_____。

⑫ 我第一次来中国，没想到_____。

⑬ 她看起来很年轻，没想到_____。

⑭ 我以为你是中国人，没想到_____。

⑮ 昨天我去逛街，真巧，_____。

⑯ A：我去找你，你怎么不在呢？

　　B：真不巧，_____。

⑰ A：这几天怎么没看到你？

B：＿＿＿＿＿＿＿＿＿＿＿＿＿＿＿＿＿＿。

A：原来是这样。

⑱ A：中国人为什么喜欢骑自行车？

B：＿＿＿＿＿＿＿＿＿＿＿＿＿＿＿＿＿＿。

A：原来是这样。

十 用"不但……，而且/还/也……"组成完整的句子。
Complete the sentences with "不但……，而且/还/也……".

A	B
会唱歌	会跳舞
我的老师	我的朋友
写汉字	写得很好
游泳	游得很快
他来	我来
他会	我会

十一 根据课文一、二的内容填空。
Fill in the blanks with the information from Texts 1 & 2.

　　卡尔来到一家银行。他先（　　），然后坐在那儿等。他想开一个储蓄（　　），这样别人可以给他（　　），他也可以随时（　　）。银行职员问他带没带（　　），并且让他（　　）了一张表。卡尔（　　）好后，（　　）了一万。他还了解到，现在欧元兑人民币的（　　）是8.83。

　　有一天，李明明在银行遇见了卡尔。卡尔来银行（　　），而李明明来银行（　　），因为她的信用卡（　　）了。银行里有很多人，他们有的（　　）水费、电费，有的买（　　）。

十二 扩展练习。

Extended exercises.

1. 办理业务　Businesses to be done

A:	你	办	什么？
B:	我	办	业务
			手续：登记手续、入学手续
			证：居留证、学生证、图书证
			卡：信用卡、饭卡、健身卡
			事

2. 交费　Make payment

A:	你	交	什么费？
B:	我	交	水费、电费、燃气费、取暖费、电话费、网费、房费
			学费、生活费、住宿费（上学费用）
			医药费、手术费、住院费、检查费（医院费用）

3. 银行列举　Bank list

A:	你	知道	中国有哪些银行？
B:	我	知道	中国人民银行
			中国银行
			中国建设银行
			中国农业银行
			中国工商银行
			民生银行
			招商银行
			交通银行

十三 阅读理解。
Reading comprehension.

　　一个中国老太太和一个美国老太太在天堂相遇。美国老太太说："我辛苦了30年，终于把住房贷款还清了。"中国老太太说："我辛苦了30年，终于攒够了买房的钱。"

生词　Shēngcí　**New Words**

1. 老太太	lǎotàitai	N	old lady
2. 天堂	tiāntáng	N	heaven
3. 相遇	xiāng yù		to encounter
4. 辛苦	xīnkǔ	Adj	hard
5. 住房	zhùfáng	N	housing
6. 贷款	dàikuǎn	N	loan
7. 清	qīng	V	with nothing left, completely
8. 攒	zǎn	V	to accumulate
9. 够	gòu	V	to reach

1. 两个老太太的故事说明了什么？
   What does the story of the two old ladies tell us?

2. 请介绍一下你们国家的消费观念。
   Talk about people's concept of consumption in your country.

3. 请根据两个老太太不同的消费观念，分成两组进行辩论。
   Divide the students into two groups and make a debate based on the different concepts of consumption of the two old ladies.

完成任务：请用课文中学过的词语和句子完成任务。
Complete the tasks: Please complete the tasks with the words and sentences you have learned in the texts.

1. 请去中国的一家银行调查下面的内容，然后在课堂上向老师和同学报告：

   Do an investigation in a bank in China and present the information you get to your teacher and classmates in class. The information to be investigated includes:

   (1) 你去的是哪家银行？去那儿做什么？

   Which bank did you go to? What did you do there?

   (2) 那家银行的顾客多不多？他们去那儿办什么业务？

   Were there many customers in the bank? What kind of transactions did they do there?

   (3) 那家银行的服务怎么样？

   How was the service in that bank?

2. 向你的中国朋友了解下面的内容，然后在课堂上报告：

   Ask your Chinese friends about the following information and make a presentation in class.

   (1) 他们有没有分期付款买过东西？买过什么东西？在哪儿买的？首付是多少？为什么选择这种方式？

   Have they ever paid by installment? For what did they pay by install-ment? Where did they buy it? How much was the down payment? Why did they choose this way of payment?

   (2) 如果你的朋友没有分期付款买过东西，请问问他们：

   If your friends have never paid by installment, then ask them the following questions:

   ① 原因；

   The reasons;

   ② 对分期付款买东西的看法；

   Their attitudes towards paying by installment;

   ③ 以后有没有分期付款买东西的打算。

   Whether they have the plan to pay by installment in the future.

第十四单元
UNIT **14**
网上购物
Shopping online

你可以网上购物
You can shop online

课文 Text	题目 Title	注释 Notes
一	你可以网上购物 You can shop online	1．表示假设关系的复句："要是……，就……" The compound sentence with "要是……，就……" denoting a suppositional relation 2．动词＋"着"（＋"也"）＋形容词 The structure "V＋着（＋也）＋Adj" 3．语气助词"呀" The modal particle "呀" 4．副词"几乎" The adverb "几乎" 5．副词"才" The adverb "才" 6．用"是不是"的正反疑问句 The affirmative-negative question with "是不是" 7．语气助词"啊" The modal particle "啊"
二	是B2B电子商务网上贸易平台吗 Is it the online trading platform for B2B electronic commerce	1．B2B（Business to Business） 2．指示代词"这样" The demonstrative pronoun "这样"
三	电子商务又省时又省力 Electronic business saves a lot of time and energy	1．"从……来看" 2．习惯用语"可不是" The idiom "可不是" 3．叹词"嘀" The interjection "嘀" 4．介词"连" The preposition "连" 5．语气助词"嘛"（复习） The modal particle "嘛"（Review）

Nǐ Kěyǐ Wǎngshang Gòu Wù

你可以网上购物

You can shop online

Kāng Àilì hé Zhāng Yuǎn zài jiàoshì li liáotiānr.

康爱丽和张远在教室里聊天儿。

Alice and Zhang Yuan are chatting in the classroom.

Kāng Àilì: Shēngcí yuè lái yuè duō le, yàoshi yǒu yí ge diànzǐ cídiǎn jiù hǎo le.

● 康爱丽: 生词越来越多了，要是有一个电子词典就好了。

Alice: There are more and more new words. How nice it will be if I have an electronic dictionary.

Zhāng Yuǎn: Shì a, diànzǐ cídiǎn chá qilai bǐjiào kuài, dàizhe yě fāngbiàn.

○ 张远: 是啊，电子词典查起来比较快，带着也方便。

Zhang Yuan: Right. It is very convenient to look up the words in an electronic dictionary, and it is easy to carry.

Kāng Àilì: Kěshì wǒ tài máng le, gēnběn méi shíjiān qù mǎi.

● 康爱丽: 可是我太忙了，根本没时间去买。

Alice: But I'm too busy to buy one.

Zhāng Yuǎn: Nǐ kěyǐ wǎngshang gòu wù a. Zàixiàn gòumǎi hái huì yǒu hěn dà de

○ 张远： 你可以网上购物啊。在线购买还会有很大的

zhékòu ne!

折扣呢！

Zhang Yuan: You can shop online, and there are big discounts.

Kāng Àilì: Shì ma? Kěshì wǒ hái bù shúxi Zhōngguó de wǎngzhàn.

● 康爱丽： 是吗？可是我还不熟悉中国的网站。

Alice: Really? But I'm still not familiar with Chinese websites yet.

Zhāng Yuǎn: Wǒ kěyǐ gàosu nǐ ya.

○ 张远： 我可以告诉你呀。

Zhang Yuan: I can tell you about it.

Kāng Àilì: Nǎge wǎngzhàn hǎo?

● 康爱丽： 哪个网站好？

Alice: Which website is better?

Zhāng Yuǎn: Táobǎo Wǎng hěn yǒumíng. Hěn duō niánqīng rén xǐhuan zài

○ 张远： 淘宝网很有名。很多年轻人喜欢在

shàngmian táo dōngxi.

上面淘东西。

Zhang Yuan: Taobao is very famous. A lot of young people like shopping on it.

Kāng Àilì: Dōu yǒu shénme?

● 康爱丽： 都有什么？

Alice: What commodities do they have?

Zhāng Yuǎn: Shénme dōu yǒu! Érqiě jīhū měi ge shāngpǐn dōu yǒu túpiàn, xuǎn

○ 张远： 什么都有！而且几乎每个商品都有图片，选

qilai hěn fāngbiàn.

起来很方便。

Zhang Yuan: Everything. Besides, nearly every commodity has its picture, so it is very

convenient to choose what you want.

Kāng Àilì: Nà tài hǎo le! Zěnme fù qián ne?

● 康爱丽： 那太好了！怎么付钱呢？

Alice: That's great! How do I pay then?

Zhāng Yuǎn: Nǐ děi xiān zài wǎngshang shēnqǐng yí ge Zhīfùbǎo zhànghù, ránhòu

○ 张远: 你得先在网上申请一个支付宝账户，然后

tōngguò wǎngshang yínháng bǎ qián zhuǎndào Zhīfùbǎo de zhànghù

通过网上银行把钱转到支付宝的账户

zhōng cái néng zhīfù.

中才能支付。

Zhang Yuan: Firstly you need to apply for an Alipay account on the Internet, and then transfer the money from your E-bank to the Alipay account. And then you can pay.

Kāng Àilì: Zhīfùbǎo? Shì bu shì hé PayPal chàbuduō?

● 康爱丽: 支付宝？是不是和PayPal差不多？

Alice: Alipay? Is it similar to PayPal?

Zhāng Yuǎn: Duì!

○ 张远: 对！

Zhang Yuan: Yes.

Kāng Àilì: Wǎngshang shūdiàn nǎ jiā hǎo?

● 康爱丽: 网上书店哪家好？

Alice: Which online bookstore is better?

Zhāng Yuǎn: Mǎi shū a、CD a、DVD a, tuījiàn nǐ shàng Dāngdāng Wǎng huòzhě

○ 张远: 买书啊、CD啊、DVD啊，推荐你上当当网或者

Zhuóyuè Wǎng.

卓越网。

Zhang Yuan: To buy books, CDs, or DVDs, dangdang.com or amazon.cn is a good option.

Kāng Àilì: Yě yòng Zhīfùbǎo ma?

● 康爱丽: 也用支付宝吗？

Alice: Do we also use Alipay?

Zhāng Yuǎn: Yǒu hěn duō zhǒng zhīfù fāngshì, yě kěyǐ huò dào fù kuǎn.

○ 张远: 有很多种支付方式，也可以货到付款。

Zhang Yuan: There are many different ways of payment, or you can pay when you get your stuff.

生词　Shēngcí　**New Words**

1. 购物	gòu wù		to go shopping
2. 越来越	yuè lái yuè		more and more
3. 要是	yàoshi	Conj	if
4. 电子	diànzǐ	N	electronic
5. 词典	cídiǎn	N	dictionary
6. 查	chá	V	to look up
7. 根本	gēnběn	Adv	at all
8. 在线	zàixiàn	V	to be online
9. 购买	gòumǎi	V	to buy
10. 折扣	zhékòu	N	discount
11. 熟悉	shúxi	V	to be familiar with
12. 网站	wǎngzhàn	N	website
13. 呀	ya	MdPt	*a modal particle for explanation or reminding*
14. 有名	yǒumíng	Adj	famous, well-known
15. 年轻	niánqīng	Adj	young
16. 淘	táo	V	to shop around (for sth.)
17. 几乎	jīhū	Adv	nearly, almost
18. 商品	shāngpǐn	N	commodity, goods
19. 图片	túpiàn	N	picture, photograph
20. 选	xuǎn	V	to choose
21. 申请	shēnqǐng	V	to apply
22. 网上银行	wǎngshang yínháng		E-bank
23. 转	zhuǎn	V	to transfer, to convey
24. 才	cái	Adv	only (then)
25. 支付	zhīfù	V	to pay

26. 推荐	tuījiàn	V	to recommend
27. 或者	huòzhě	Conj	or
28. 货到付款	huò dào fù kuǎn		a means of payment (especially for the online shopping), meaning that the buyer can pay after he/she receives the stuff and makes confirmation
货	huò	N	goods

专有名词 Zhuānyǒu Míngcí **Proper Nouns**

1. 淘宝网	Táobǎo Wǎng	taobao.com, an online shopping website
2. 支付宝	Zhīfùbǎo	alipay.com, an online payment platform
3. 当当网	Dāngdāng Wǎng	dangdang.com, an online shopping website
4. 卓越网	Zhuóyuè Wǎng	amazon.cn, an online shopping website

注释 Zhùshì **Notes**

1 要是有一个电子词典就好了。**How nice it will be if I have an electronic dictionary.**

"要是……，就……"，表示假设关系的复句。"要是"，连词，表假设，意思是"如果，如果是"。"要是"用在前一分句时，后一分句常用"就"。口语中，助词"的话"可以和"要是"配合使用，放在前一分句句末。"要是"后除了带小句，还可以单独带代词、名词或动词。例如：

The structure "要是……，就……" is a compound sentence indicating a suppositional relation. "要是", a conjunction, means "if", with the similar meaning to "如果" and "如果是". "要是" is used in the first clause to raise a supposition, and in the latter clause "就" is usually used to show the possible result under the supposition. In spoken Chinese, the auxiliary "的话" can be used together with "要是" and put at the end of the first clause. Besides a clause, "要是" can also be followed by a pronoun, a noun or a verb. For example,

① 你要是看见《法汉词典》，就帮我买一本。

② 要是有人打电话找我的话，就说我不在。

③ 要是我就不会去。

④ 要是不来北京，怎么能认识你呢？

汉语中还常固定在后一分句用"就好了"表示结果，组成"要是 + 小句 + 就好了"，也表示说话人的愿望。例如：

In Chinese, "就好了" is often used in the latter clause to compose the structure "要是 + clause + 就好了" to indicate a result, which is also the wish of the speaker. For example,

Conj（要是）	clause	就好了
要是	我有很多钱	就好了。
	张远能来	
	明天是个晴天	

2 **电子词典查起来比较快，带着也方便。**

It is very convenient to look up the words in an electronic dictionary, and it is easy to carry.

"动词 + 着（+ 也）+ 形容词"结构。其中，形容词表示动作的状态、结果；动词一般是单音节的；形容词前常常带副词"也"，承接上一句对主语的描述，说明主语另一方面的性质。例如：

The adjective in the structure "verb + 着（+ 也）+ adjective" indicates the state or result. The verb is usually monosyllabic and the adjective is often proceeded by "也" to connect the description of the subject in the previous sentence and to introduce another property of the subject. For example,

① 这张沙发很便宜，坐着也舒服。

② 这件衣服不贵，穿着也好看。

③ 老师今天讲的语法不难，学着容易。

3 **我可以告诉你呀。** I can tell you about it.

"呀"，语气助词，读轻声，是"啊"的音变。"啊"用在句末或句中时，发音常受前一个字韵母或韵尾的影响而发生不同的变音。变音后可以用原字，也可以写成不同的字。具体规律见下表：

"呀", a modal particle with the neutral tone, is the alternative pronunciation of "啊". When the auxiliary "啊" is used at the end or in the middle of a sentence, its pronunciation is often inflected under the influence of the final of the word before it. "啊" can be either reserved or changed into a different one (see the table below).

前一个字的韵母或韵尾 The final of the previous character	"啊"的发音和写法 The pronunciation and writing of "啊"
a、e、i、o、ü	a→ia　呀
u、ao、ou	a→ua　哇
-n	a→na　哪
-ng	a→nga　啊

例如：
For example,

陈述句 Declarative sentence	啊/呀/哇/哪
我去找爸爸（ba）	呀/啊
你去学一学（xué）	呀/啊
你可以在网上买（mǎi）	呀/啊
他想找的人是我（wǒ）	呀/啊
我们走路去（qù）	呀/啊
我们走路（lù）	啊/哇
你会跳舞（wǔ）	啊/哇
这个小区很安全（quán）	啊/哪
我想请你帮忙（máng）	啊

4 **而且几乎每个商品都有图片，选起来很方便。**

Besides, nearly every commodity has its picture, so it is very convenient to choose what you want.

"几乎"，副词，表示非常接近。可以用在动词、形容词、名词、句子前。本句中"几乎"就放在句子"每个商品都有图片"前。例如：

"几乎", an adverb, means "nearly" and can be put before verbs, adjectives, or sentences. In this sentence, "几乎" is put before the sentence "每个商品都有图片". For example,

① 他高兴得几乎跳了起来。

② 这两本书几乎一样厚。

③ 我们班几乎所有的学生都喜欢王老师。

5 **然后通过网上银行把钱转到支付宝的账户中才能支付。**

Transfer the money from your E-bank to the Alipay account, and then you can pay.

"才"，副词，表示"只有在某种条件下，或由于某种原因、目的，然后怎么样"。用于后一小句，前一小句常有"只有、必须"或是含有这种意思的词语，构成"只有……才……"的结构，表示这个条件是唯一的。这里，"把钱转到支付宝的账户中"是条件，"支付"是结果。这个句子可以改成："只有通过网上银行把钱转到支付宝的账户中，才能用支付宝来支付。"例如：

"才", an adverb, indicates that something happens only under a certain condition or for a certain reason and purpose. With "才" used in the latter clause and "只有", "必须" or a word with the similar meaning used in the previous one, the structure "只有……才……" indicates that this condition is the only one. In the given sentence, "把钱转到支付宝的账户中" is the condition and "支付" is the result. Therefore, this sentence can be changed into "只有通过网上银行把钱转到支付宝的账户中，才能用支付宝来支付。" For example,

① 站得高才能看得远。
② 只有办了银行卡或存折，才能转账。
③ 现在太晚了，必须打车去才来得及。

6 是不是和 **PayPal** 差不多？ Is it similar to PayPal?

正反疑问句。这里是动词"是"的肯定形式和它的否定形式"不是"组成的正反疑问句。当问话人对某一事实或情况有了比较肯定的估计并希望进一步证实时，就可以用这种疑问句来提问。"是不是"可以放在句首、句末或谓语前。这种疑问句要求听话人对事实的真假作出回答。例如：

This is an affirmative-negative question with "是不是". This kind of sentence is often used by an asker who has an affirmative estimation of some situation and wants to get a further confirmation. "是不是" can be put at the beginning or the end of a sentence, or before the predicate of a sentence. The affirmative-negative question is used when the asker needs the listener to give an answer about whether something is true or false. For example,

① 是不是你们不打算回国？
② 后天有考试，是不是？
③ 他爸爸是不是在美国？

7 买书啊、CD啊、DVD啊，…… To buy books, CDs, or DVDs, ...

"啊"，语气助词，读轻声，用在列举的事项之后。例如：

"啊", a modal particle, with the neutral tone, is used after each of the listed items. For example,

① 苹果啊，香蕉啊，草莓啊，他买了很多水果。
② 这件衣服的颜色啊、款式（kuǎnshì, style）啊、大小啊，都很合适。

Shì B2B Diànzǐ Shāngwù Wǎngshang Màoyì Píngtái ma

是B2B电子商务网上贸易平台吗

Is it the online trading platform for B2B electronic commerce

Kāng Àilì hé Zhāng Yuǎn zài jiǔbā liáotiānr.

康爱丽和张远在酒吧聊天儿。

Alice and Zhang Yuan are chatting in the bar.

Kāng Àilì:　　Gōngsī zǒngbù ràng wǒmen zài Zhōngguó xúnzhǎo fúzhuāng

● 康爱丽：　　公司总部让我们在中国寻找服装

　　　　　　shēngchǎn chǎngjiā. Nǐ yǒu shénme jiànyì?

　　　　　　生产厂家。你有什么建议？

Alice:　　　The Headquarters make us find clothing manufacturers in China. Do you

　　　　　　have any suggestions?

Zhāng Yuǎn: Nǐ kěyǐ shàng "Ālǐbābā" wǎngzhàn kànkan.

○ 张远：　　　你可以上"阿里巴巴"网站看看。

Zhang Yuan: You can take a look at the website of "alibaba".

Kāng Àilì:　　Shì B2B diànzǐ shāngwù wǎngshang màoyì píngtái ma?

● 康爱丽：　　是B2B电子商务网上贸易平台吗？

Alice:　　　Is it the online trading platform for B2B electronic commerce?

Zhāng Yuǎn: Shì. Zhōngguó hěn duō qǐyè dōu shì tā de yònghù, dōu zài shàngmian
○ 张远：　是。中国很多企业都是它的用户，都在上面
fābù chǎnpǐn xìnxī、xúnzhǎo kèhù.
发布产品信息、寻找客户。
Zhang Yuan: Yes. Lots of enterprises in China are its clients. They issue information on
their products and search for clients on it.

Kāng Àilì: Nà wǎngzhàn shang yīnggāi yǒu qǐyè de liánxì fāngshì ba?
● 康爱丽：　那网站上应该有企业的联系方式吧？
Alice: There should be the contact information of the enterprises, right?

Zhāng Yuǎn: Dāngrán. Zhèyàng, nǐmen jiù kěyǐ hé chǎngjiā zhíjiē liánxì le,
○ 张远：　当然。这样，你们就可以和厂家直接联系了，
duì ba?
对吧？
Zhang Yuan: Sure. Then you can contact the manufacturers directly, right?

Kāng Àilì: Duì. Zhèr jiù yǒu diànnǎo, zánmen shàngqu kànkan ba. Wǎngzhǐ shì
● 康爱丽：　对。这儿就有电脑，咱们上去看看吧。网址是
shénme?
什么？
Alice: Yes. Here is the computer. Let's have a look. What's the website?

Zhāng Yuǎn: www.alibaba.com.
○ 张远：　www.alibaba.com。
Zhang Yuan: www.alibaba.com.

Kāng Àilì: Děng yíxià, wǒ jì yíxià.
● 康爱丽：　等一下，我记一下。
Alice: Wait a minute. Let me write it down.

生词 Shēngcí **New Words**

1. 电子商务	diànzǐ shāngwù		electronic commerce
2. 贸易	màoyì	N	trade, business
3. 平台	píngtái	N	platform

4. 总部	zǒngbù	N	headquarters
5. 寻找	xúnzhǎo	V	to seek, to look for
6. 服装	fúzhuāng	N	clothing
7. 生产	shēngchǎn	V	to produce, to manufacture
8. 厂家	chǎngjiā	N	factory, manufacturer
9. 企业	qǐyè	N	enterprise
10. 用户	yònghù	N	client, user
11. 发布	fābù	V	to issue
12. 产品	chǎnpǐn	N	product
13. 信息	xìnxī	N	information
14. 联系	liánxì	V	to contact
15. 直接	zhíjiē	Adj	direct
16. 网址	wǎngzhǐ	N	website address
17. 记	jì	V	to write down, to note

专有名词 Zhuānyǒu Míngcí **Proper Noun**

| 阿里巴巴 | Ālǐbābā | the name of a commercial website |

注释 Zhùshì **Notes**

1 是B2B电子商务网上贸易平台吗?

Is it the online trading platform for B2B electronic commerce?

B2B,Business to Business,是商家对商家的电子商务,是电子商务发展过程中的一种交易模式。有时写成 B to B,但人们已经习惯用它的谐音形式 B2B(2 是 two,与 to 同音)。B2B 是指进行电子商务交易的供需双方都是商家(企业或公司),他们使用互联网技术或各种商务网络平台完成商务交易过程，具体包括：发布供求信息，货比三家，讨价还价，订货及确认订货，支付过程及票据的签发、传送和接收，确定配送方案并监控配送过程等。比如"阿里巴巴"就是面向中间交易市场的 B2B 商务平台，它把各个行业中相近的交易过程集中到一个场所，为企业的采购方和供应方提供交易的机会。

B2B, short for "Business to Business", is the enterprise-to-enterprise e-commerce which is a trading mode during the development of e-commerce. Sometimes it is written as "B to B", but people have got used to its partial tone "B2B". In B2B, both the supplying and demanding sides of the e-commercial trading are enterprises (companies) which complete the commercial trading process by using the Internet technologies or various kinds of commercial network platforms. The commercial trading process includes issuing the supplying and demanding information, comparing the qualities and prices of the commodities, bargaining, ordering and ordering confirmation, paying and signing, transmitting and receiving of the invoice, confirming the distributing plan, and monitoring the distributing process, etc. For example, Alibaba is a B2B oriented towards the intermediate trading market, which gathers the similar trading processes of various industries to one place and supplies both the purchasers and suppliers with good trading opportunities.

2 这样，你们就可以和厂家直接联系了。

Then you can contact the manufacturers directly.

"这样"，指示代词，指示性质、状态、方式和程度等。"这样"可以用在句中或句首，起到承接上文、引出下文的连接作用。"这样"后面的句中常用"就"。例如：

"这样", a demonstrative pronoun, indicates property, state, means or degree, etc. "这样" can be put in the middle or at the beginning of a sentence to play the function of connecting the following text with the previous one. "就" is often used in the sentence following "这样". For example,

① 多听、多说，这样，你就可以很快地提高你的汉语水平了。

② 卡尔帮我把电脑修好了，这样，我就可以上网聊天儿了。

③ 现在有了"网上广交会（Guǎngjiāohuì, Canton Fair）"，这样，很多厂家就不用去广州了。

Diànzǐ Shāngwù Yòu Shěngshí Yòu Shěnglì

电子商务又省时又省力

Electronic business saves a lot of time and energy

Kāng Àilì hé Zhāng Yuǎn zài liáotiānr.

康爱丽和张远在聊天儿。

Alice and Zhang Yuan are chatting.

Kāng Àilì: Shàng cì wǒmen zài wǎngshang zhǎo de nà jǐ ge chǎngjiā, wǒ yǐjīng

● 康爱丽: 上次我们在网上找的那几个厂家，我已经

liánxìguo le.

联系过了。

Alice: I've contacted the manufacturers we found from the Internet last time.

Zhāng Yuǎn: Shì ma? Zěnme yàng?

○ 张远: 是吗？怎么样？

Zhang Yuan: Really? How is that?

Kāng Àilì: Cóng wǎngshang de túpiàn lái kàn, yǒu liǎng ge chǎngjiā de chǎnpǐn

● 康爱丽: 从网上的图片来看，有两个厂家的产品

hái búcuò, bàojià yě bǐjiào dī.

还不错，报价也比较低。

Alice: From the pictures on the Internet, we know there are two manufacturers that have good products and also offer low prices.

Zhāng Yuǎn: Yào bu yào qù shídì kǎochá?

○ 张远： 要不要去实地考察？

Zhang Yuan: Will you make an on-site inspection?

Kāng Àilì: Háishi yīnggāi shídì kǎochá yíxià, bǐjiào bǎoxiǎn.

● 康爱丽： 还是应该实地考察一下，比较保险。

Alice: An on-site inspection is necessary. It's safer.

Zhāng Yuǎn: Qiānyuē yǐhòu, jiù kěyǐ tōngguò wǎngluò gěi tāmen xià dìngdān le.

○ 张远： 签约以后，就可以通过网络给他们下订单了。

Zhang Yuan: After signing the contract, you can place the order to them via Internet.

Kāng Àilì: Kě bu shì. Diànzǐ shāngwù yòu shěngshí yòu shěnglì.

● 康爱丽： 可不是。电子商务又省时又省力。

Alice: Right. Electronic business saves a lot of time and energy.

Zhāng Yuǎn: Yǐqián zuò guójì màoyì, shénme shìr zuì ràng rén tóuténg?

○ 张远： 以前做国际贸易，什么事儿最让人头疼？

Zhang Yuan: What was the biggest headache in the international trade before?

Kāng Àilì: Xúnzhǎo màoyì huǒbàn.

● 康爱丽： 寻找贸易伙伴。

Alice: Searching for trading partners.

Zhāng Yuǎn: Nàge shíhou liánxì qilai yě hěn máfan ba?

○ 张远： 那个时候联系起来也很麻烦吧？

Zhang Yuan: Was it also difficult to make contacts at that time?

Kāng Àilì: Shì a, zhǐ néng dǎ diànhuà、fā chuánzhēn, érqiě hái yǒu shíchā de

● 康爱丽： 是啊，只能打电话、发传真，而且还有时差的

wèntí.

问题。

Alice: Yes. Telephone and fax were the only ways. And time difference was also a problem.

Zhāng Yuǎn: Qù guówài chūchāi chéngběn yě hěn gāo.

○ 张远: 去国外出差成本也很高。

Zhang Yuan: It also cost much to go abroad for a business trip.

Kāng Àilì: Méi cuò!

● 康爱丽: 没错！

Alice: Absolutely.

Zhāng Yuǎn: Duì le, Guǎngzhōu zhèngzài jǔbàn "Zhōngguó Jìn-chūkǒu Shāngpǐn

○ 张远: 对了，广州正在举办"中国进出口商品

Jiāoyìhuì".

交易会"。

Zhang Yuan: Oh, China Import and Export Fair is being held in Guangzhou right now.

Kāng Àilì: Nǐ shì shuō "Guǎngjiāohuì" ba? Wǒmen yǐjīng dēnglùguo

● 康爱丽: 你是说"广交会"吧？我们已经登录过

"Wǎngshang Guǎngjiāohuì", kànguo cānzhǎn chǎngjiā de xìnxī le,

"网上广交会"，看过参展厂家的信息了，

suǒyǐ búyòng qù Guǎngzhōu le.

所以不用去广州了。

Alice: You mean Canton Fair? We have logged on the Online Canton Fair and seen the information of the exhibiting enterprises, so we don't even need to go to Guangzhou.

Zhāng Yuǎn: Hē, nǐ lián chūchāifèi dōu shěng le!

○ 张远: 嗬，你连出差费都省了！

Zhang Yuan: Oh, the cost for the business trip is also saved!

Kāng Àilì: Jīngjì wēijī, jiéyuē chéngběn ma!

● 康爱丽: 经济危机，节约成本嘛！

Alice: As we have the economic crisis, we should try to decrease the cost!

生词　Shēngcí　New Words

1. 省	shěng	V	to save
2. 力	lì	N	energy, force

3. 报价	bàojià	N	quotation, quoted price
4. 实地	shídì	Adv	on-site
5. 考察	kǎochá	V	to investigate, to inspect
6. 保险	bǎoxiǎn	Adj	safe, secure
7. 签约	qiān yuē	V//O	to sign a contract
8. 订单	dìngdān	N	order sheet
9. 可不是	kě bu shì		absolutely *(expressing agreement)*
10. 国际	guójì	Adj/N	international
11. 伙伴	huǒbàn	N	partner
12. 传真	chuánzhēn	N/V	fax; to fax
13. 时差	shíchā	N	time difference
14. 成本	chéngběn	N	(manufacturing, production, etc.) cost
15. 进出口	jìn-chūkǒu		import and export
进口	jìn kǒu	V//O	to import
出口	chū kǒu	V//O	to export
16. 交易	jiāoyì	N/V	transaction; to trade
17. 登录	dēnglù	V	to log on
18. 参展	cānzhǎn	V	to participate in an exhibition
19. 嗬	hē	Int	oh
20. 连	lián	Prep	even
21. 危机	wēijī	N	crisis
22. 节约	jiéyuē	V	to economize, to save

专有名词 Zhuānyǒu Míngcí **Proper Nouns**

| 1. 广州 | Guǎngzhōu | name of a Chinese city |
| 2. 中国进出口商品交易会 | Zhōngguó Jìn-chūkǒu Shāngpǐn Jiāoyìhuì | China Import and Export Fair |

| 3. 广交会 | Guǎngjiāohuì | Canton Fair *(another name of China Import and Export Fair)* |

注释　Zhùshì　**Notes**

1 从网上的图片来看，有两个厂家的产品还不错。

From the pictures on the Internet, we know there are two manufacturers that have good products.

"从……来看"，由介词"从"和"来看"组成的常用格式，意思是"从……方面看问题"。"从"引出的是论述的依据，下文是由此推出的某种结论和判断。例如：

"从……来看" is a structure often used composed of "从" and "来看". "从" is used to bring out the basis of the discussion, and the following text is the deduced conclusion or judgment. For example,

① 从他的身体情况来看，他还不能开始工作。

② 从这一点来看，她是我们班最努力的学生。

③ 从报价来看，我们应该和他们公司签约。

2 可不是。Right.

"可不是"，习惯用语，在对话中用来回应对方，表示附和、赞同对方的话。也可以说"可不、可不是嘛"。例如：

"可不是", an idiom, is used when the speaker agrees with the other party. "可不" or "可不是嘛" can also be used. For example,

A	B
听说你们最近生意不错。	可不是，现在市场很火。
现在有了网络，做事真方便。	可不是嘛，又省时又省力。
咱们明天该去看看王老师了。	可不（是），很长时间没去了。

3 嘀，你连出差费都省了！ Oh, the cost for the business trip is also saved!

"嘀"，叹词，表示惊讶等。例如：

"嘀", an interjection, indicates a surprise. For example,

① 嗬，你们公司好大呀！

② 嗬，康爱丽今天穿得真漂亮！

③ 嗬，这么多人！

4 **你连出差费都省了。** **The cost for the business trip is also saved!**

"连"，介词，表示强调，常和"都、也"连用，组成"连……都 / 也……"结构，有"甚至于"的意思。"连"后可跟代词、名词、动词、数量词、小句等组成介宾短语。例如：

"连", a preposition, is used for emphasis. It forms the structure of "连……都/也……" with "都" or "也", meaning "even". "连" can be followed by a pronoun, a noun (NP), a verb (VP), a numeral-classifier compound or a clause to form a preposition-object phrase. For example,

S	P			
	Prep（连）	O	Adv（都/也）	V
这件事	连	我	都	知道了。
我		见	都	没见过。（1）
我		他住在哪儿	也	忘了问。（2）
他		试卷上错了几个字	都	记得。（2）
我们		一个字	都	没说。（3）

注意： **Note：**

（1）"连+动词"时，谓语限于否定形式（有时前后为同一动词）。

In "连 + verb", the predicate should be in the negative form (sometimes the verb after "连" is the same as the predicate verb).

（2）"连 + 小句"时，小句由疑问代词或不定数词构成。

In "连 + clause", the clause is made up of an interrogative pronoun or a non-specific numeral.

（3）"连 + 数量词"时，数词一般为"一"，谓语用否定形式。

In "连 + numeral-classifier compound", the numeral is usually "一", and the predicate should be in the negative form.

5 **经济危机，节约成本嘛！**

As we have the economic crisis, we should try to decrease the cost!

"嘛"，语气助词，用在陈述句或小句末尾，表示事情本该如此或道理显而易见，加强肯定语气。我们在第七单元课文二中已经学过。用"嘛"的小句前后常有表示原因或其他说明情况的小句。如课文中的"经济危机"就是说明"节约"的原因。注意：表示疑问语气用

"吗"，不用"嘛"。例如：

"嘛", a mood auxiliary, used at the end of an affirmative sentence or a clause, indicates that something is just as what it should be or a truth can tell its own tale. It strengthens the affirmative tone. We have learned it in Text 2 of Unit 7. There is often another clause before or after the clause with "嘛" to explain the reason or other situation. In the given sentence, "经济危机" is the reason for "节约". "嘛" doesn't indicate an interrogative mood, while "吗" does. For example,

① 我们公司的生意本来就好嘛。

② 你去问她嘛，她一定知道。

③ 他是经理嘛，当然得他作决定。

练习　Liànxí　**Exercises**

一　跟读生词，注意发音和声调。
Read the new words after the teacher and pay attention to your pronunciation and tones.

二　跟读课文，注意语音语调。
Read the texts after the teacher and pay attention to your pronunciation and intonation.

三　学生分组，分角色朗读课文一、二、三。
Divide the students into groups and read Texts 1, 2 & 3 in different roles.

四　学生分组，不看书，分角色表演课文一、二、三。
Divide the students into groups and play the roles in Texts 1, 2 & 3 without referring to the book.

五　角色扮演。（提示：角色可以互换。）
Role playing. (Note: the roles can be exchanged.)

1. 两个学生一组，互相询问是不是在网上买过东西，买了什么。用课文里学过的词语和句子完成一段对话。

   Work in pairs and ask your partner whether he / she shopped online before and what he / she has bought. Make a dialogue with the words and sentences that have been learned from the texts.

2. 两个学生一组，接着上面的话题一起聊一聊：
   Work in pairs and have a talk following the above topic.

   （1）你们所知道的网上购物的支付方式有哪些？怎么支付？

   What kinds of paying methods do you know for shopping online? What are they?

   （2）你认为哪种支付方式最方便？为什么？

   Which paying method do you think is the most convenient? Why?

六　复述课文二。
Retell Text 2.

七 替换练习。
Substitution drills.

① 生词　越来越　多　了。

我的电脑	慢
我们的合作厂家	多
电子商务网站	专业（zhuānyè, professional）
卡尔	爱吃中国饭
我	不懂

② 要是　有一个电子词典　就好了。

能找到服装生产厂家

我是经理

康爱丽在这儿

不用排队

我能参加你们的拓展训练

③ 电子词典查起来比较快，带　着　也方便。

这款手机的样子很好看	用	也方便
这件衣服很便宜	穿	也舒服
这块手表康爱丽	戴	好看
儿子买的房子，他	住	高兴
记住老师告诉你的方法	练	不累

④ 几乎　每个商品都有图片。

跟中国人的发音一样

等了你两个小时

每个人都去开会了

听不见

⑤每　个　商品　都　有图片。

个	经理	有一个秘书
张	照片	是回忆（huíyì, memory）
个	月	得上班
个	员工	要去培训（péixùn, to train）

⑥然后通过网上银行把钱转到支付宝的账户中　才　能支付。

只有领了号	能办业务
要多练习	能发好音
只有他来做	能成功
多运动	能身体好

⑦公司总部　让　我们　在中国寻找服装生产厂家。

张远	请	卡尔	帮忙
老板	让	康爱丽	上网查查
卡尔	教	王老师	打网球
经理	叫	他	去上班
公司	派	小王	去法国总部出差
老师	鼓励	我们	好好学习

⑧你　可以　上"阿里巴巴"网站　看看。

你	去那个公司	问一问
咱们	在这个酒吧	聊聊
卡尔	到我家	住几天
咱们	和他们	认识认识

9 从 <u>网上的图片</u> 来看，有两个厂家的产品还不错。

他的外貌（wàimào, appearance）	我很难猜出他的年纪
外贸服装现在的市场	这个报价比较合适
质量	这个厂家的产品不错
她的身体情况	她已经可以回来上班了

10 你 连 <u>出差费</u> 都 <u>省了</u>。

我	银行卡密码	告诉你了
他们	饭	没吃
我	听说	没听说
他	"阿里巴巴"	不知道

八 用下面的词语组成句子。
Make sentences with the following words and expressions.

1 电子词典　起来　比较　查　快

2 在线购买　有　呢　会　折扣　还　很大的

3 东西　很多　喜欢　上面　年轻人　在　淘

4 你　申请　一个　先　得　支付宝账户　在网上

5 网站　应该　联系方式　上　有　企业　的

6 就　通过网络　下订单　可以　给他们　你　了

7 商务　省时　又　电子　省力　又

⑧ 出差　成本　去　也　国外　很高

⑨ 过　"网上广交会"　我们　登录　已经　了

九 用 "应该、可以、能、得、会" 填空（可多选）。
Choose one word or more from "应该", "可以", "能", "得" or "会" to fill in the blanks.

① A：明天他＿＿＿＿＿＿去上班吗？

　　B：＿＿＿＿＿＿去。

② 您好，我＿＿＿＿＿＿进来吗？

③ 明天有考试，卡尔＿＿＿＿＿＿准备准备。

④ 张远明天一定＿＿＿＿＿＿来上班。

⑤ 你＿＿＿＿＿＿去网上查一查。

⑥ 他＿＿＿＿＿＿说日语和英语。

⑦ 明天＿＿＿＿＿＿下雨。

⑧ 我们＿＿＿＿＿＿想想怎么办。

十 阅读理解。
Reading comprehension.

（一）

　　康爱丽学习汉语已经四个月了。现在，课本中的生词越来越多，她很想买一个电子词典。可是她最近很忙，根本没时间去商店。张远告诉她可以在网上买，又便宜又方便。后来康爱丽真的在淘宝网上买了一个电子词典，还买了一些传统的工艺品。她觉得在网上买东西不受时间限制，而且可以买到北京没有的东西，方便极了。

生词	Shēngcí	**New Words**	
1. 传统	chuántǒng	Adj	traditional
2. 工艺品	gōngyìpǐn	N	handicraft
3. 受	shòu	V	to be subjected to
4. 限制	xiànzhì	N	limitation

回答问题：

Answer the questions:

1 康爱丽学汉语多长时间了？

2 康爱丽为什么想买一个电子词典？

3 张远建议康爱丽怎么做？

4 康爱丽在哪儿买的电子词典？

5 康爱丽还买了什么？

6 康爱丽觉得网上购物怎么样？

（二）

　　上个月，法国总部给康爱丽写了一封邮件，让她在中国找一个服装生产厂家。康爱丽上"阿里巴巴"网站看了看，并且和几个厂家联系了。虽然从网上的图片来看，有两个生产厂家的产品还不错，不过康爱丽还是想去实地考察一下。她也登录过"网上广交会"，看过参展厂家的信息。现在是经济危机，她想节约一些出差成本。

回答问题：

Answer the questions:

1 康爱丽是什么时候收到法国总部的邮件的？

2 法国总部让康爱丽做什么？

3 康爱丽是怎么找服装生产厂家的？

4 她找到合适的生产厂家了吗？

5 康爱丽打算去广州参加"广交会"吗？

十一 完成任务：请用课文中学过的词语和句子完成任务。
Complete the tasks: Please complete the tasks with the words and sentences you have learned in the texts.

1. 请试着在本文介绍的购物网站上购买一样东西，然后向老师和同学介绍你的购物经历及感受。

   Try to buy something on the Internet as recommended by this unit and present to your teacher and classmates your shopping experience and feeling.

2. 请登录"阿里巴巴"网站，找到一个服装生产厂家的介绍和联系方式，然后向老师和同学介绍你了解到的情况。

   Visit the website of Alibaba, find the information about a clothing manufacturer and its contact information, and then present the information you get to your teacher and classmates.

希望您在这儿过得愉快
Wish you a good time here

课文 Text	题目 Title	注释 Notes
一	我想预订房间 I'll like to reserve a room	1. 征询语及礼貌用语 The inquiring expressions and polite expressions 2. 动词"需要" The verb "需要" 3. 动词"帮助" The verb "帮助" 4. 副词"大约" The adverb "大约" 5. 动词"差" The verb "差" 6. 敬辞"贵" The term of respect "贵" 7. 介词"按" The preposition "按" 8. 形容词"紧张" The adjective "紧张"
二	你打算怎么安排 What arrangement will you make for him	1. 副词"将" The adverb "将" 2. 动词"希望" The verb "希望" 3. 连词"此外" The conjunction "此外" 4. 副词"极" The adverb "极" 5. 介词"为" The preposition "为" 6. 介词"由" The preposition "由"
三	您有什么需要尽管说 Please don't hesitate to tell me whenever you need help	1. 副词"尽管" The adverb "尽管" 2. "有朋自远方来，不亦乐乎！" 3. 结构助词"地" The structural particle "地"

Wǒ Xiǎng Yùdìng Fángjiān

我想预订房间

I'll like to reserve a room

客房预订部

Kāng Àilì de lǎo kèhù Màikè yào lái Běijīng chūchāi, tā xīwàng Kāng Àilì néng wèi tā ānpái yí cì shāngwù zhī lǚ. Kāng Àilì de mìshū Xiǎo Qián zhèngzài gěi Sìhǎi Dà Jiǔdiàn dǎ diànhuà.

康爱丽的老客户麦克要来北京出差，他希望康爱丽能为他安排一次商务之旅。康爱丽的秘书小钱正在给四海大酒店打电话。

Mike, Alice's regular client, will come to Beijing for a business trip and he hopes that Alice can arrange this trip for him. Xiao Qian, Alice's secretary, is making a call to Sihai Hotel.

Zǒngjī: Nín hǎo! Sìhǎi Dà Jiǔdiàn!

● 总机：   您好！四海大酒店！

Telephone exchange of Sihai Hotel: Good morning! This is Sihai Hotel.

Xiǎo Qián: Nín hǎo!

○ 小钱：   您好！

Xiao Qian: Good morning!

Zǒngjī: Qǐngwèn nín yǒu shénme xūyào bāngzhù de?

● 总机： 请问您有什么需要帮助的？

Telephone exchange of Sihai Hotel: Can I help you?

Xiǎo Qián: Wǒ xiǎng yùdìng fángjiān.

○ 小钱： 我想预订房间。

Xiao Qian: I'll like to reserve a room.

Zǒngjī: Wǒ bāng nín zhuǎn Kèfáng Yùdìngbù.

● 总机： 我帮您转客房预订部。

Telephone exchange of Sihai Hotel: I'll help you get through to the Department of Room Reservation.

Diànhuà zhuǎnjiē zhōng.

电话转接中。

The call is being transferred.

Fúwùyuán: Nín hǎo! Sìhǎi Dà Jiǔdiàn Kèfáng Yùdìngbù.

○ 服务员： 您好！四海大酒店客房预订部。

Waitress: Good morning! This is the Department of Room Reservation, Sihai Hotel.

Xiǎo Qián: Nín hǎo! Wǒ xiǎng yùdìng fángjiān.

● 小钱： 您好！我想预订房间。

Xiao Qian: Good morning! I'll like to reserve a room.

Fúwùyuán: Nín jǐ wèi? Dǎsuàn jǐ hào rùzhù? Zhù jǐ tiān?

○ 服务员： 您几位？打算几号入住？住几天？

Waitress: Can I ask how many guests, when to check in, and how long will the guests stay?

Xiǎo Qián: Yí wèi, xià zhōurì, sìyuè èrshíliù hào xiàwǔ rùzhù, dàyuē zhù yì zhōu.

● 小钱： 一位，下周日，4月26号下午入住，大约住一周。

Xiao Qian: Only one. He will check in on the afternoon of next Sunday, April 26th, and will stay for about one week.

Fúwùyuán: Èrshíliù、èrshíqī hào shì sānbǎi qīshíbā yì tiān, yǐhòu shì liùbǎi bāshí,

○ 服务员： 26、27号是378一天，以后是680，

jiā shōu bǎi fēnzhī shíwǔ de fúwùfèi.

加收15%的服务费。

Waitress: 378 *yuan* per day for 26th and 27th, and 680 *yuan* per day for the rest of the days, plus 15% service fee.

Xiǎo Qián: Zhè shì biāozhǔnjiān de jiàgé ma?
● 小钱： 这是标准间的价格吗？
Xiao Qian: Is this the price of a standard room?

Fúwùyuán: Shì de.
○ 服务员： 是的。
Waitress: Yes.

Xiǎo Qián: Nà xíngzhèngjiān ne?
● 小钱： 那行政间呢？
Xiao Qian: What about an executive room?

Fúwùyuán: Sìbǎi jiǔshíbā、bābǎi wǔshí，jiā shōu bǎi fēnzhī shíwǔ de fúwùfèi.
○ 服务员： 498、850，加收 15% 的服务费。
Waitress: 498 and 850, plus 15% service fee.

Xiǎo Qián: Qiánhòu de jiàgé zěnme chà zhème duō? Hán zǎocān ma?
● 小钱： 前后的价格怎么差这么多？含早餐吗？
Xiao Qian: Why is there so large a difference? Is breakfast included?

Fúwùyuán: Bù hán zǎocān. Xiànzài shì lǚyóu wàngjì，jiàgé shàngtiáo le.
○ 服务员： 不含早餐。现在是旅游旺季，价格上调了。
Waitress: Breakfast is not included. It is the tourist season now, so the price has been raised.

Xiǎo Qián: Wǒmen gōngsī shì guì jiǔdiàn de hézuò dānwèi，àn xiéyì kěyǐ xiǎngshòu
● 小钱： 我们公司是贵酒店的合作单位，按协议可以享受
wǔ zhé yōuhuì.
5 折优惠。
Xiao Qian: Our company is your hotel's partner. According to our contract, we can get a 50% discount.

Fúwùyuán: Zhè shì tèjià，bǐ xiéyìjià hái piányi. Xiànzài biāozhǔnjiān hěn jǐnzhāng，
○ 服务员： 这是特价，比协议价还便宜。现在标准间很紧张，
búguò，wǒmen kěyǐ yōuxiān ānpái guì gōngsī de kèrén.
不过，我们可以优先安排贵公司的客人。
Waitress: This is a special offer and it is even lower than the contracted price. The standard rooms are in short supply now, but we can offer you a priority to make an arrangement for the guest from your company.

Xiǎo Qián: Qǐng bǎ jiàmùbiǎo chuánzhēn gěi wǒmen ba.
● 小钱： 请把价目表传真给我们吧。
Xiao Qian: Please fax me the price list.

Fúwùyuán: Hǎo de. Nín de chuánzhēn hàomǎ shì duōshao?
○ 服务员： 好的。您的传真号码是多少？
Waitress: OK. Can you tell me your fax number?

Xiǎo Qián: Liù yāo èr sān sì wǔ liù qī.
● 小钱： 61234567。
Xiao Qian: 61234567.

Fúwùyuán: Xièxie, zàijiàn!
○ 服务员： 谢谢，再见！
Waitress: Thank you. Goodbye.

Xiǎo Qián: Zàijiàn!
● 小钱： 再见！
Xiao Qian: Goodbye.

生词　Shēngcí　New Words

1. 总机	zǒngjī	N	telephone exchange
2. 需要	xūyào	V	to need
3. 帮助	bāngzhù	V	to help
4. 客房	kèfáng	N	guest room
5. 大约	dàyuē	Adv	about
6. 加收	jiā shōu		plus
7. 服务费	fúwùfèi	N	service fee
8. 标准间	biāozhǔnjiān	N	standard room
9. 价格	jiàgé	N	price
10. 行政间	xíngzhèngjiān	N	executive room
11. 差	chà	V	to differ from

12. 含	hán	V	to include
13. 上调	shàngtiáo	V	to raise
14. 酒店	jiǔdiàn	N	hotel
15. 单位	dānwèi	N	an organization
16. 按	àn	Prep	according to
17. 协议	xiéyì	N	contract
18. 享受	xiǎngshòu	V	to enjoy
19. 优惠	yōuhuì	Adj	favorable
20. 特价	tèjià	N	special offer
21. 紧张	jǐnzhāng	Adj	in short supply
22. 优先	yōuxiān	V	to have priority
23. 价目表	jiàmùbiǎo	N	price list

专有名词　Zhuānyǒu Míngcí　Proper Noun

| 四海大酒店 | Sìhǎi Dà Jiǔdiàn | Sihai Hotel |

注释　Zhùshì　Notes

1　**请问您有什么需要帮助的？　Can I help you?**

礼貌用语，是服务行业的人员在询问顾客需求时用的。在酒店行业有些常用的礼貌用语，其中包括一些征询语。例如：

This sentence is often used by people in the service trade to ask about the needs of their customers. The commonly used polite expressions, including some inquiring expressions, are listed below.

征询语 Inquiring expressions	我能为您做什么吗？ 需要我帮您做什么吗？ 请问您有什么事？ 您还有别的事吗？ 您喜欢 / 需要 / 能够……？ 请您……，好吗？
其他常用礼貌用语 Commonly used polite expressions	请、您、您好、您早、早上好、晚上好、谢谢、不客气、对不起、请原谅、没关系、打扰您了 欢迎光临！ / 欢迎您来我们酒店。 路上辛苦了！ 欢迎您下次再来！ / 再见！

2 **请问您有什么需要帮助的？ Can I help you?**

"需要"，这里是动词，表示应该有或者必须有。可以带名词、动词、形容词、小句宾语。可以受程度副词的修饰，不能重叠。例如：

"需要", a verb here, indicates somebody should or must have something. It can be followed by a noun, a verb, an adjective or a clause as the object and can be modified by a degree adverb, but can't be reduplicated. For example,

S	P		
	A	V（需要）	O
我们大家	都	需要	你。　　　　　　　（Pr）
我		需要	你的帮助。　　　　（NP）
他	非常	需要	休息。　　　　　　（V）
公司		需要	我们去上海考察。（sentence）

"需要"也是名词，表示一种欲望和要求。可以作主语和宾语，必须带修饰语。例如：

"需要" can also be a noun, indicating a desire or a need. It can serve either as the subject or as the object, and must have a modifier. For example,

① 孩子们的需要是我们最关心的。

② 他没有这样的需要。

3 请问您有什么需要帮助的？ Can I help you?

"帮助"，动词，可以带名词、代词宾语。"帮助"的宾语可以作兼语，但不能作"帮助"后面的动词的定语。例如：

"帮助", a verb, can be followed by a noun or a pronoun as the object, which can also serve as the linkage but cannot serve as the attribute of the verb after "帮助". For example,

① 他帮助我学习。（ √ ）

（"我"是兼语，既是"帮助"的宾语，又是"学习"的主语 Being a pivot, "我" is the object of "帮助" and the subject of "学习".）

② 他帮助我的学习。（ × ）

③ 大家要帮助明明/她。

④ 张远帮助卡尔做作业。

4 大约住一周。He will stay for about one week.

"大约"，副词，表示估计的数目不是很精确，句中一般有数字。可以作状语，但不能在名词前作定语。例如：

"大约", an adverb, indicates the estimated number is not precise. There should be a number in the sentence. "大约", as an adverbial modifier, cannot be put before a noun as the attribute. For example,

① 他们大约有十几个人。

② 现在大约几点了？

③ 卡尔大约 9 月回国。

5 前后的价格怎么差这么多？ Why is there so large a difference (in price)?

"差"，动词，表示"不相同、相差"。不单独作谓语，可带名词宾语，也可带补语。例如：

"差", a verb, means "to differ". It cannot serve as predicate individually, but can be followed by a noun as the object, and can also take a complement. For example,

① 我的汉语水平跟你比差远了。

② 这两家酒店的条件（tiáojiàn, condition）差得很多。

③ 这两个国家的发展速度（sùdù, speed）差了几十年。

"差"还是形容词，表示"不好，不够标准"。例如：

"差", can also be an adjective, indicating something is not good, or has not reached the standard. For example,

④ 他的考试成绩很差。

⑤ 他们公司的产品质量很差。

6 我们公司是贵酒店的合作单位。Our company is your hotel's partner. / 我们可以优先安排贵公司的客人。We can offer you a priority to make an arrangement for the guest from your company.

"贵",敬辞,称呼与对方有关的事物,表示尊敬和礼貌。在商务交往中,"贵"常放在表示组织、机构、单位等概念的词语前,也是一种商务礼仪。例如:"贵公司、贵厂、贵校、贵国"等。需要注意的是,"贵"不能放在"家"前,要表达类似的意思,可用"贵府(fǔ, mansion house)"一词。

"贵", a term of respect, is used to address something that is related to the other party to show one's respect or courtesy. It is also a kind of business etiquette. In business communication, "贵" is often put before the word denoting organization, institution or enterprise, such as "贵公司", "贵厂", "贵校", and "贵国", etc. What should be noted is that "贵" cannot be put before "家". To express the similar meaning, "贵府" can be used.

7 按协议可以享受 5 折优惠。According to our contract, we can get a 50% discount.

"按",介词,用来引出要遵守的标准、规定或条件,可以带名词、动词、小句组成介宾短语作状语。例如:

"按", a preposition, is used to bring out the standard, stipulation or condition to be followed. It can be followed by a noun, a verb or a clause to form a prepositional phrase as an adverbial modifier. For example,

① 你最好按约定的时间去。

② 老师按成绩把新同学分成了四个班。

③ 我们应该按老师的要求去做。

8 现在标准间很紧张。The standard rooms are in short supply now.

"紧张",形容词,这里是"供应不足,难于应付"的意思。可以作谓语,不能重叠。例如:

"紧张", an adjective, indicates something is in short supply. It can serve as the predicate, but can't be reduplicated. For example,

① 现在是旅游旺季,火车票很紧张。

② 今年市场上的猪肉供应(gōngyìng, to supply)不紧张,就是有点儿贵。

Nǐ Dǎsuàn Zěnme Ānpái

你打算怎么安排

What arrangement will you make for him

Kāng Àilì hé tā de mìshū Xiǎo Qián zhèngzài
shāngliang Màikè zài Běijīng de xíngchéng ānpái.

康爱丽和她的秘书小钱正在商量麦克在北京的
行程安排。

Alice and her secretary Xiao Qian are discussing the schedule of
Mike in Beijing.

Kāng Àilì: Xiǎo Qián, Màikè lái Zhōngguó de xíngchéng fā guolai le ma?

● 康爱丽： 小钱，麦克来中国的行程发过来了吗？

Alice: Xiao Qian, has Mike sent us his schedule in China?

Xiǎo Qián: Fā guolai le. Màikè jiāng zài Běijīng tíngliú yì zhōu, ránhòu qù

○ 小钱： 发过来了。麦克将在北京停留一周，然后去

Shànghǎi, cóng Shànghǎi huí guó.

上海，从上海回国。

Xiao Qian: Yes. Mike will stay in Beijing for a week, then go to Shanghai, and then
leave China from Shanghai.

Kāng Àilì: Tā yǒu shénme yāoqiú?

● 康爱丽： 他有什么要求？

Alice: Does he have any requests?

Xiǎo Qián: Zài Běijīng, chúle gōngzuò zhīwài, tā xīwàng zánmen néng dài tā qù

○ 小钱： 在北京，除了工作之外，他希望咱们能带他去

cānguān yíxià míngshèng gǔjì. Cǐwài, tā hái xiǎng gěi péngyou mǎi xiē

参观一下名胜古迹。此外，他还想给朋友买些

lǐwù.

礼物。

Xiao Qian: Besides work, he hopes that we can take him to visit some places of historic interest and scenic beauty in Beijing. In addition, he wants to buy some presents for his friends.

Kāng Àilì: Nǐ dǎsuàn zěnme ānpái?

● 康爱丽： 你打算怎么安排？

Alice: What arrangement will you make for him?

Xiǎo Qián: Sìhǎi Dà Jiǔdiàn, sì xīngjí, jiàgé bǐ tónglèi jiǔdiàn piányi. Wǒ xiǎng

○ 小钱： 四海大酒店，四星级，价格比同类酒店便宜。我想

bāng tā zài nàr yùdìng fángjiān.

帮他在那儿预订房间。

Xiao Qian: Sihai Hotel, a four-star hotel, is cheaper than others of the same kind. I want to reserve a room for him there.

Kāng Àilì: Zhōuwéi huánjìng zěnmeyàng?

● 康爱丽： 周围环境怎么样？

Alice: What about its surrounding environment?

Xiǎo Qián: Jiù zài Àoyùn chǎngguǎn de pángbiān. Zhèyàng, yì chūmén jiù kěyǐ

○ 小钱： 就在奥运场馆的旁边。这样，一出门就可以

kàndào Niǎocháo hé Shuǐlìfāng.

看到鸟巢和水立方。

Xiao Qian: It's near the Olympic stadium and gymnasium. The moment he walks out of the hotel, he can see the Bird's Nest and the Water Cube.

Kāng Àilì: Hǎojí le!

● 康爱丽： 好极了！

Alice: That's great!

Xiǎo Qián: Dìng biāozhǔnjiān háishi xíngzhèngjiān ne? Zhè shì jiàmùbiǎo.

○ 小钱: 订标准间还是行政间呢？这是价目表。

Xiao Qian: Shall we reserve a standard room or an executive one? Here is the price list.

Kāng Àilì: Jiù dìng xíngzhèngjiān. Nǐ jìhuà dài tā qù nǎxiē dìfang?

● 康爱丽: 就订行政间。你计划带他去哪些地方？

Alice: An executive one. What places do you plan to take him to?

Xiǎo Qián: Zhè shì wǒ wèi Màikè nǐdìng de huódòng rìchéngbiǎo, qǐng nín

○ 小钱: 这是我为麦克拟定的活动日程表，请您

guòmù.

过目。

Xiao Qian: This is the itinerary I've made for Mike. Please have a look.

Kāng Àilì kànwánle rìchéngbiǎo.

康爱丽看完了日程表。

Alice finishes looking at the itinerary.

Kāng Àilì: Nǐ shì Běijīng rén, shúxi huánjìng, jiù yóu nǐ lái péitóng ba.

● 康爱丽: 你是北京人，熟悉环境，就由你来陪同吧。

Alice: You are a Beijinger and familiar with this city, so can you accompany him?

Xiǎo Qián: Hǎo de.

○ 小钱: 好的。

Xiao Qian: OK.

Kāng Àilì: Ānpái hǎo chē jiējī le ma?

● 康爱丽: 安排好车接机了吗？

Alice: Have you arranged the car to meet him at the airport?

Xiǎo Qián: Ānpái hǎo le.

○ 小钱: 安排好了。

Xiao Qian: Yes, I have.

Kāng Àilì: Nǐ gēn wǒ yíkuàir qù.

● 康爱丽: 你跟我一块儿去。

Alice: You can go with me.

生词　Shēngcí　**New Words**

1. 安排	ānpái	V	to arrange
2. 将	jiāng	Adv	will
3. 停留	tíngliú	V	to stay
4. 要求	yāoqiú	N	request
5. 希望	xīwàng	V	to hope
6. 名胜古迹	míngshèng gǔjì		place of historic interest and scenic beauty
7. 此外	cǐwài	Conj	in addition
8. 四星级	sì xīngjí		four-star
9. 同类	tónglèi	Adj	of the same kind
10. 周围	zhōuwéi	N	surrounding
11. 奥运	Àoyùn	N	Olympic Games
12. 场馆	chǎngguǎn	N	stadium and gymnasium
13. 出门	chū mén	V//O	to go out
14. 极	jí	Adv	extremely
15. 计划	jìhuà	V/N	to plan; plan
16. 为	wèi	Prep	for
17. 拟定	nǐdìng	V	to make, to work out
18. 日程表	rìchéngbiǎo	N	schedule, itinerary
19. 过目	guò mù	V//O	to have a look
20. 由	yóu	Prep	by
21. 陪同	péitóng	V	to accompany
22. 接机	jiē jī	V//O	to meet sb. at the airport
23. 一块儿	yíkuàir	Adv	together

专有名词 Zhuānyǒu Míngcí **Proper Nouns**

1. 麦克	Màikè	Mike
2. 鸟巢	Niǎocháo	Bird's Nest (Beijing National Stadium / Olympic Stadium)
3. 水立方	Shuǐlìfāng	Water Cube (The National Aquatics Center)

注释 Zhùshì **Notes**

1 **麦克将在北京停留一周。** **Mike will stay in Beijing for a week .**

"将"，副词，表示动作或情况不久就会发生，"将要"的意思。在句中修饰动词，可以作状语。当动词前有介词结构时，"将"一般放在介词结构前。例如：

"将", an adverb, indicates that an action or situation will take place before long, similar to "将要". As an adverbial modifier, it modifies the verb in the sentence. When there is a prepositional structure before the verb, "将" is usually put before the prepositional structure. For example,

① 他将在12月22日回国。

② 后年我们将去美国工作。

③ 明明将在下周二晚上举办生日聚会。

2 **他希望咱们能带他去参观一下名胜古迹。**

He hopes that we can take him to visit some places of historic interest and scenic beauty.

"希望"，动词，表示心里想达到某种目的或出现某种情况。可以带代词、动词和小句宾语，不能带补语，不能重叠。例如：

"希望", a verb, indicates somebody hopes that some goal can be reached or some situation can take place. It can be followed by a pronoun, a verb or a clause as the object, but it cannot be followed by a complement, nor can it be reduplicated. For example,

① 我一直希望能来中国工作。

② 她希望你能参加她的生日聚会。

③ 王经理希望下周去上海考察。

3 此外，他还想给朋友买些礼物。In addition, he wants to buy some presents for his friends.

"此外"，连词，表示除了前面所说的事情或情况之外的。当"此外"后面是肯定形式时，表示除了前面所说的还有别的，后面的句子中常用"还、也"；当"此外"后面是否定形式时，表示除了前面所说的没有别的。"此外"可以连接句子或小句，常用在书面语中。例如：

"此外", a conjunction, means "besides the aforesaid thing or situation". When "此外" is followed by an affirmative sentence, it indicates that there is still something else besides what is aforesaid, and "还" or "也" is often used in the following sentence. When "此外" is followed by a negative sentence, it indicates that there is nothing else besides what is aforesaid. "此外" can connect sentences or clauses and is usually used in written language. For example,

① 我们班有德国人、法国人，此外，还有西班牙人。

② "十一"黄金周我们去了上海、南京、杭州、苏州，此外，没去别的地方。

③ 康爱丽的办公室里有一张桌子、一把椅子和一组沙发，此外再没有别的了。

4 好极了！That's great!

"极"，副词，表示达到最高程度。可以作补语，但是前面不能用"得"，后面一般带"了"，放在形容词和少数动词的后面。例如：

"极", an adverb, indicates the highest degree. It can be used as a complement, but can't be put after "得". It is often put after adjectives or a few verbs, and is usually followed by "了". For example,

① 这里的风景美极了！

② 这家饭馆的菜难吃极了！

③ 这家酒店的床舒服极了！

5 这是我为麦克拟定的活动日程表，请您过目。

This is the itinerary I've made for Mike. Please have a look.

"为"，介词，表示行为的对象，可以带名词、代词组成介词短语作状语，修饰动词。例如：

"为", a preposition, brings out the object of the action. It can be followed by nouns or pronouns to form a prepositional structure serving as an adverbial modifier to modify the verb. For example,

① 卡尔为明明买了生日礼物。

② 我很希望能为你们公司做点儿事。

③ 我们很高兴能为您服务。

6 就由你来陪同吧。Can you accompany him?

"由"，介词，表示某事归某人去做，引进动作的施事。例如：

"由", a preposition, indicates that something should be done by someone. It is used to bring out the agent of the action. For example,

① 这次会议由他安排。

② 这份计划将由王经理来为我们介绍。

③ 今天的晚餐就由我来买单。

您有什么需要尽管说

Nín Yǒu Shénme Xūyào Jǐnguǎn Shuō

Please don't hesitate to tell me
whenever you need help

Màikè gēnsuí Kāng Àilì、Xiǎo Qián cóng jīchǎng
láidào jiǔdiàn de fángjiān. Fànghǎo xíngli, Xiǎo
Qián bǎ rìchéngbiǎo gěi Màikè.

麦克跟随康爱丽、小钱从机场来到酒店的房间。
放好行李，小钱把日程表给麦克。

Mike gets to the hotel from the airport with Alice and Xiao Qian.
Xiao Qian gives the itinerary to him after he puts away his baggage.

Xiǎo Qián: Zhè shì nín zhè jǐ tiān de xíngchéng ānpái, zhè shì nín qù Shànghǎi de

● 小钱： 这是您这几天的行程安排，这是您去上海的

huǒchēpiào.

火车票。

Xiao Qian: This is your itinerary in Beijing, and this is your train ticket to Shanghai.

Màikè: Hǎo de.

○ 麦克： 好的。

Mike: OK.

Xiǎo Qián: Hái yǒu，wǒ yǐjīng qǐng wǒmen Shànghǎi fēngōngsī de tóngshì

● 小钱： 还有，我已经请我们上海分公司的同事

jiēzhàn le.

接站了。

Xiao Qian: And I have asked my colleague in our Shanghai branch to meet you when you arrive in Shanghai.

Màikè： Xièxie nǐ!

○ 麦克： 谢谢你!

Mike: Thank you.

Xiǎo Qián: Bú kèqi! Nín yǒu shénme xūyào jǐnguǎn shuō. Zhè shì wǒ de míngpiàn,

● 小钱： 不客气! 您有什么需要尽管说。这是我的名片，

shàngmian yǒu wǒ de diànhuà.

上面有我的电话。

Xiao Qian: You are welcome. Please don't hesitate to tell me whenever you need help. This is my card and my telephone number is on it.

Màikè： Hǎo de. Àilì, Xiǎo Qián zhēn nénggàn!

○ 麦克： 好的。爱丽，小钱真能干!

Mike: OK. Alice, Xiao Qian is really a capable girl.

Xiǎo Qián: Xièxie nín! Zhōngguó yǒu jù gǔhuà:"Yǒu péng zì yuǎnfāng lái, bú yì lè

● 小钱： 谢谢您! 中国有句古话："有朋自远方来，不亦乐

hū!" Wǒmen zhēnchéng de xīwàng nín zài zhèr guò de yúkuài.

乎!"我们真诚地希望您在这儿过得愉快。

Xiao Qian: Thank you! There is an old saying in China—"It is such a delight to have friends coming from afar." We sincerely wish you a good time in China.

Màikè： Xièxie!

○ 麦克： 谢谢!

Mike: Thank you.

Kāng Àilì: Màikè, nǐ xiàwǔ jiù xiūxi xiūxi ba, wǎnshang liù diǎn wǒmen lái jiē

● 康爱丽： 麦克，你下午就休息休息吧，晚上 6 点我们来接

nǐ, zài jiǔdiàn de cāntīng wèi nǐ jiēfēng xǐchén!

你，在酒店的餐厅为你接风洗尘!

Alice: Mike, you can have a rest this afternoon. We will come to meet you at 6:00 p.m. and treat you a dinner of welcome in the dining hall of the hotel.

Màikè:　　 Hǎo de. Wǎnshang jiàn!

○ 麦克：　　 **好的。晚上见！**

Mike:　　 OK. See you this evening!

Kāng Àilì、Xiǎo Qián: Wǎnshang jiàn!

● 康爱丽、小钱：　　 **晚上见！**

Alice and Xiao Qian:　 See you this evening!

附：麦克在北京的日程表

时　间	行　程
4月26日（周日）	下午1点到达北京；入住四海大酒店； 参观奥运场馆。 晚饭，四海大酒店餐厅。
4月27日（周一）~ 4月29日（周三）	在北京工作、开会。
4月30日（周四）	上午，去长城； 午饭，长城脚下的饭馆； 下午，去地安门附近的胡同（坐三轮车）； 晚饭，后海附近的饭馆； 饭后去酒吧。
5月1日（周五）	上午，去故宫； 午饭，前门大栅栏附近的饭馆； 下午，去北海； 晚宴，北海公园里的仿膳饭庄。
5月2日（周六）	上午，去天坛； 午饭，天坛附近的饭馆； 下午，红桥市场购物。 晚宴，前门的全聚德。
5月3日（周日）	上午，酒店退房后可以去颐和园参观或者去秀水街购物（二选一）； 午饭，景点附近的饭馆； 晚饭，北京站附近的饭馆； 晚上7点，送站； 晚上8点，坐火车去上海，第二天早上9点到上海。

Attached: Mike's Itinerary in Beijing

Date	Itinerary
April 26 (Sun.)	1. Arrive in Beijing at 1:00 p.m.; check in at Sihai Hotel; a visit the Olympic stadium and gymnasium. 2. Have dinner in the dining hall of Sihai Hotel.
April 27 ~ 29 (Mon. ~Wed.)	Work and attend meetings in Beijing.
April 30 (Thur.)	1. Go to the Great Wall in the morning; 2. Have lunch in the restaurant at the Great Wall; 3. Go to the Hutong near Di'anmen by tricycle; 4. Have supper in a restaurant near Houhai; 5. Go to a bar after supper.
May 1 (Fri.)	1. Go to the Palace Museum in the morning; 2. Have lunch in a restaurant near Qianmen Dashilar; 3. Go to Beihai Park in the afternoon; 4. Have supper in Fangshan Restaurant in Beihai Park.
May 2 (Sat.)	1. Go to the Temple of Heaven in the morning; 2. Have lunch in a restaurant near the Temple of Heaven; 3. Go shopping in Hongqiao Market in the afternoon; 4. Have supper in Quanjude in Qianmen.
May 3 (Sun.)	1. After checking out, pay a visit to the Summer Palace or go shopping in Xiushui Street; 2. Have lunch in a restaurant nearby; 3. Have supper in a restaurant near Beijing Railway Station; 4. See off Mike at 7:00 p.m.; 5. Mike gets on the train at 8:00 p.m. and will arrive in Shanghai at 9:00 a.m. the next day.

生词 Shēngcí New Words

1. 尽管	jǐnguǎn	Adv	despite
2. 火车	huǒchē	N	train
3. 票	piào	N	ticket
4. 分公司	fēngōngsī	N	branch company
5. 接站	jiē zhàn	V//O	to meet sb. at the railway station
6. 能干	nénggàn	Adj	capable, able
7. 古话	gǔhuà	N	old saying
8. 自	zì	Prep	from, since
9. 远方	yuǎnfāng	N	a distant place
10. 亦	yì	Adv	also, too
11. 乎	hū	Pt	*an exclamatory particle that expresses doubt or indicates a rhetorical question*
12. 真诚	zhēnchéng	Adj	sincere
13. 地	de	StPt	*an auxiliary particle used after an adjective or a phrase to form an adverbial modifier before the verb*
14. 愉快	yúkuài	Adj	happy
15. 接风洗尘	jiēfēng xǐchén		to give a dinner of welcome

注释 Zhùshì Notes

1 **您有什么需要尽管说。** **Please don't hesitate to tell me whenever you need help.**

"尽管"，副词，这里表示不必考虑别的，放心去做。可以用在动词前，作状语，常用于口语中。例如：

"尽管", an adverb, indicates that somebody can do something without thinking of or worrying about anything. It can be put before a verb as the adverbial modifier, and is often used in spoken Chinese. For example,

① 你们有问题尽管问。

② 你有什么想法，尽管说。

2 中国有句古话："有朋自远方来，不亦乐乎！"

There is an old saying in China—"It is such a delight to have friends coming from afar."

"有朋自远方来，不亦乐乎"，出自中国古代著作《论语》，是著名教育家、思想家孔子所说，一直沿用至今。今天人们常用这句话来表达"朋友来了很高兴"的意思。

This sentence is extracted from the ancient masterpiece *The Analects of Confucius,* which collects the words of Confucius, the great educationalist and ideologist. People today use this sentence to express their happiness to see their friends coming from afar.

3 我们真诚地希望您在这儿过得愉快。We sincerely wish you a good time in China.

"地"，结构助词，放在中心语之前，表示它前面的词或短语是状语。一般描写性的状语都要用"地"。例如：

"地", an auxiliary, put before the head word, indicates that the word or phrase before it is an adverbial modifier. "地" is always used after an adverbial modifier which is of descriptive function. For example,

S	P		
	Adj/V	StPt（地）	V/VP
他们	愉快		交谈着。
我们	真诚	地	祝您成功！
大家	静静		等着。
雪	不停		下。

注意：Note：

（1）一般单音节形容词后不能用"地"；数量短语后也不能用"地"。例如：

Generally, a monosyllabic adjective, a monosyllabic adverb or a numeral-clssifier compound cannot be followed by "地". For example,

① 他看着我傻笑。（√）

② 他看着我傻地笑。（×）

③ 他一下子买了十本书。（√）

④ 他一下子地买了十本书。（×）

（2）除少数单音节形容词以外，形容词作状语且前面有程度副词时，要用"地"。例如：

Except for a small number of monosyllabic adjectives, "地" should be used when there is an adverb denoting degree before the adjective serving as an adverbial. For example,

⑤ 这句话很难懂。（√）

⑥ 这句话很难地懂。（×）

⑦ 他们很高兴地走了。（√）

⑧ 他很客气地说出了自己的要求。（√）

练习 Liànxí **Exercises**

一 跟读生词，注意发音和声调。
Read the new words after the teacher and pay attention to your pronunciation and tones.

二 跟读课文，注意语音语调。
Read the text after the teacher and pay attention to your pronunciation and intonation.

三 学生分组，分角色朗读课文一、二、三。
Divide the students into groups and read Texts 1, 2 & 3 in different roles.

四 学生分组，不看书，分角色表演课文一、二、三。
Divide the students into groups and play the roles in Texts 1, 2 & 3 without referring to the book.

五 角色扮演。（提示：角色可以互换。）
Role playing. (Note: the roles can be exchanged.)

1. 两人一组，一人扮演酒店客房预订部员工 A，一人扮演客人 B，B 给 A 打电话预订房间。用课文中学过的词语和句子完成一段对话。
Two students work as a group. One acts as A who works in the Room Reservation Department of a hotel, and the other acts as the guest B. B calls A to reserve a room. Make a dialogue with the words and sentences that have been learned from the texts.

B 需要询问：房间的种类、价格、房间的设施（如能否上网，可根据自己的实际情况提出要求）、折扣情况等。
B is supposed to ask for the following information: the types of rooms, the prices, the facilities in the room (for example, whether there's access to the Internet, and you can make a request according to your own need), and discount, etc.

A 要一一给出回答，同时也应该询问：客人的人数、入住的时间、对房间的设施有什么要求、对预订房间的要求等。
A is supposed to give all the answers and ask B at the same time about: the number of the guests, the check-in time, the request for the facilities in the room, and other requests for the room to be reserved.

2. 两人（A 和 B）一组，假设两人的朋友 C 来 A、B 所在的城市出差，有几天假期要和 A、B 一起过。A 和 B 商量：如何一起接待 C、如何安排这几天的假期。可以设想 C 的要求和爱好，根据这些来安排行程。用课文中学过的词语和句子完成一段对话。
Two students act as A and B. Their friend C will come to their city on a business trip and have a several days' holiday to spend with them together. A and B have a discussion together about

how they will treat C and what arrangement they will make for this holiday. Please assume C's requests and hobbies, and work out an itinerary based on his requests and hobbies. Make a dialogue with the words and sentences that have been learned from the texts.

六 复述课文三。
Retell Text 3.

七 替换练习。
Substitution drills.

① 麦克 大约 住一周。

教室里	有二十几个人
从北京到上海	一千多公里
坐火车去上海	要 10 个小时
期末考试	在 12 月底举行
现在	6 点了

② 前后的价格 怎么差这么多?

我们公司的管理	差在哪儿
你们俩的汉语成绩	差多少
德国和法国的发展速度	差得不多
老师的看法和我们的	差得很远
他们的年龄	差了 8 岁

③ 我们 按 协议 可以享受 5 折优惠。

	约定	你可以 8 点钟来
你应该	时	上课
我们是	老师的要求	做的
你们能	咱们谈好的价格	支付吗
他为什么不	月	交房租

147

④ 下周　麦克　将　在北京　停留一周。

明年5月	我		去法国工作
	明明	在下周二	举办生日聚会
	你们	在哪儿	结婚
	他们	在什么时候	回国
	公司	请谁	来当总经理
今年10月	公司	在北京	举办经济研讨会

⑤ 他　很　希望　咱们　能带他去参观名胜古迹。

我	非常		能和你一起工作
妈妈		明明	去英国留学
我		你	有空儿锻炼锻炼身体
父母		他们	早点儿买房子
老板		康爱丽	能实地考察生产厂家

⑥ 这是我　为　麦克　拟定的活动日程表。

张远	康爱丽的公司	找到了合作伙伴
我们很高兴能	您	服务
她	她的先生	买了一件生日礼物
卡尔	他的客户	介绍了德国总公司的情况
你能	她	唱一首歌吗
你在	谁	工作
他为什么要	你	写诗（shī, poem）

⑦ <u>麦克</u> 就 由 <u>你</u> 来陪同吧。

麦克		小钱	接待
金龙公司		林琳	当总经理
会议报告	已经	我的秘书	送走了
这份计划	应该	张经理	来为我们介绍
今天的午餐	就	我	来买单吧

⑧ <u>您有什么需要</u> 尽管 <u>说</u>。

你喜欢什么	买
你们有问题	问
你有什么要求	写
你们有意见	提（tí, to mention）
这些蛋糕很好吃，	吃
这些饮料是免费（miǎn fèi, to be free of charge）的，	喝

⑨ <u>我们真诚</u> 地 <u>希望您在这儿过得愉快</u>。

他们高兴	见了面
我们生气	离开了
他们努力	学习
妈妈幸福（xìngfú, happy）	笑了

八 用下面的词语组成句子。

Make sentences with the following words and expressions.

① 的 您 请问 有 需要 帮助 什么

② 入住 几号 打算

③ 服务费　　的　　15%　　加收

④ 合作　　我们　　单位　　贵酒店　　公司　　是　　的

⑤ 吗　　了　　发过来　　的　　来中国　　麦克　　行程

⑥ 在那儿　　房间　　帮他　　预订　　我想

⑦ 怎么样　　环境　　周围

⑧ 订　　呢　　还是　　行政间　　标准间

⑨ 地方　　去　　计划　　哪些　　带他　　你

⑩ 已经请　　的　　上海分公司　　同事　　我　　我们　　接站了

⑪ 吧　　就　　休息　　下午　　你　　休息

⑫ 接风洗尘　　餐厅　　酒店　　为你　　在　　我们　　的

九 阅读理解。
Reading comprehension.

　　康爱丽的老客户麦克要来北京出差，除了工作以外，他还有四天的假期。他希望康爱丽能为他安排在北京的酒店和这四天的旅行。康爱丽让她的秘书小钱安排。

　　小钱联系了四星级的四海大酒店。虽然现在是旅游旺季，但这是他们公司的合作酒店，可以优先安排他们的客人。小钱把计划好的日程表给她的老板过目。康爱丽满意倒是满意，就是觉得日程安排得有点儿满，应该给麦克留出一点儿时间供他自由支配。不过，她没有让小钱改，只是让她把日程发给麦克，没有问题就马上安排。

生词　Shēngcí　**New Words**

1. 老	lǎo	Adj	old
2. 假期	jiàqī	N	holiday
3. 支配	zhīpèi	V	to arrange
4. 改	gǎi	V	to change

回答问题：

Answer the questions:

① 谁要来北京？他来北京做什么？

② 他让康爱丽帮他做什么？

③ 小钱联系了什么样的酒店？

④ 康爱丽对小钱的计划满意吗？为什么？

⑤ 康爱丽让小钱改计划了吗？她让小钱怎么做？

 完成任务：请用课文中学过的词语和句子完成任务。

Complete the tasks: Please complete the tasks with the words and sentences you have learned in the texts.

---

1. 两人或三人一组，假设某位组员的一位朋友要来这里，请根据他／她的要求和爱好选定一家酒店。准备好你们希望了解的问题，然后试着给这家酒店打电话或者去这家酒店的前台询问。此外，请去这家酒店实地考察一下它的环境。

Two or three students work as a group. Suppose a friend of one of the group members is coming to your city and you are asked to select a hotel for him / her according to his / her request. Prepare the questions you will ask and try to give this hotel a call or go to the front desk of the hotel for consultation. Besides, please go to this hotel to make an on-site investigation on the surrounding environment.

要了解的问题包括：房间的价格、设施、可以提供哪些服务等。请把你们了解和考察的情况记录下来，然后在上课时向老师和同学报告。

What you need to know includes: the price of the room, the facilities and the services available, etc. Please make a note of the information you get, and present it to your teacher and classmates in class.

2. 两人或三人一组，假设某位组员的一位朋友要来北京几天（具体时间可以自己确定）。根据你们对北京的了解，为你们的朋友设计一份在北京旅行的日程表，并在课堂上向老师和同学介绍，同时说明为什么这样安排。

Two or three students work as a group. Suppose that a friend of one of the group members is coming to Beijing for several days (you may decide the time). Please make an itinerary for him / her according to your knowledge about Beijing, and present it to your teacher and classmates in class and explain why you make such arrangement at the same time.

生词总表
Vocabulary

（最后一列表示生词所在单元和课号，如"132"表示第十三单元课文二）

（The last column indicates the unit number and text number of the new word, for example, "132" indicates the new word is in Text 2, Unit 13.）

A					
1	安排	ānpái	V	to arrange	152
2	按	àn	Prep	according to	151
3	奥运	Àoyùn	N	Olympic Games	152
B					
4	把	bǎ	Prep	*used to bring out the patient of a verb*	112
5	把	bǎ	M	*a measure word*	123
6	白板	báibǎn	N	whiteboard	123
7	摆	bǎi	V	to put	123
8	拜托	bàituō	V	to request a favour	121
9	办	bàn	V	to do, to handle	131
10	办公室	bàngōngshì	N	office	123
11	办公桌	bàngōngzhuō	N	desk, bureau	123
12	帮助	bāngzhù	V	to help	151
13	包括	bāokuò	V	to consist of, to include	122
14	保安	bǎo'ān	N	safeguard	131
15	保险	bǎoxiǎn	Adj	safe, secure	143
16	报价	bàojià	N	quotation, quoted price	143
17	报纸	bàozhǐ	N	newspaper	123
18	爆	bào	V	to explode	132
19	被	bèi	Prep	by *(expression of passive voice)*	114

20	本	běn	N	notebook	111
21	鼻涕	bítì	N	snot	112
22	笔记本电脑	bǐjìběn diànnǎo		laptop	133
23	标准间	biāozhǔnjiān	N	standard room	151
24	表	biǎo	N	form	131
25	病	bìng	N/V	illness; to be ill	112
26	病历	bìnglì	N	medical record, case history	111

C

27	才	cái	Adv	only (then)	141
28	菜市场	càishìchǎng	N	food market	121
29	参展	cānzhǎn	V	to participate in an exhibition	143
30	茶几	chájī	N	tea table	123
31	查	chá	V	to look up	141
32	差	chà	V	to differ from	151
33	产品	chǎnpǐn	N	product	142
34	厂家	chǎngjiā	N	factory, manufacturer	142
35	场馆	chǎngguǎn	N	stadium and gymnasium	152
36	朝	cháo	V	to face	123
37	车位	chēwèi	N	parking space	122
38	成本	chéngběn	N	(manufacturing, production, etc.) cost	143
39	出差	chū chāi	V//O	to go on a business trip	112
40	出口	chū kǒu	V//O	to export	143
41	出门	chū mén	V//O	to go out	152
42	出租	chūzū	V	to rent out	121
43	厨房	chúfáng	N	kitchen	121
44	储蓄	chǔxù	V	to deposit	131
45	传真	chuánzhēn	N/V	fax; to fax	143

46	窗户	chuānghu	N	window	123
47	窗口	chuāngkǒu	N	window	131
48	窗台	chuāngtái	N	window sill	123
49	词典	cídiǎn	N	dictionary	141
50	此外	cǐwài	Conj	in addition	152
51	存	cún	V	to deposit	131
52	存款	cúnkuǎn	N	deposit, savings deposit	131
53	存折	cúnzhé	N	deposit book	131

D

54	大厦	dàshà	N	building, edifice	122
55	大约	dàyuē	Adv	about	151
56	大夫	dàifu	N	doctor	111
57	带	dài	V	to carry, to take, to bring	131
58	单位	dānwèi	N	an organization	151
59	但是	dànshì	Conj	but	123
60	倒是	dàoshì	Adv	*used to indicate concession*	121
61	地	de	StPt	*an auxiliary particle used after an adjective or a phrase to form an adverbial modifier before the verb*	153
62	登录	dēnglù	V	to log on	143
63	等	děng	Pt	and so on, etc.	132
64	地上	dìshàng	N	on the ground	122
65	地下	dìxià	N	underground	122
66	电	diàn	N	electricity	122
67	电子	diànzǐ	N	electronic	141
68	电子商务	diànzǐ shāngwù		electronic commerce	142
69	订单	dìngdān	N	order sheet	143
70	定期	dìngqī	Adj	fixed (deposit)	131

71	肚子	dùzi	N	stomach, belly	113
72	对面	duìmiàn	N	the opposite side	123
73	兑	duì	V	to exchange	131

F

74	发布	fābù	V	to issue	142
75	发愁	fā chóu	V//O	to be worried	121
76	发烧	fā shāo	V//O	to have a fever	112
77	发炎	fāyán	V	to inflame	112
78	方式	fāngshì	N	method, way	133
79	房间	fángjiān	N	room	123
80	房租	fángzū	N	rent	121
81	放	fàng	V	to put	123
82	费	fèi	N	expense, fee	111
83	分公司	fēngōngsī	N	branch company	153
84	分期	fēnqī	V	by installment	133
85	服务费	fúwùfèi	N	service fee	151
86	服装	fúzhuāng	N	clothing	142
87	付	fù	V	to pay	121
88	付款	fù kuǎn		to pay	133

G

89	干净	gānjìng	Adj	clean	121
90	赶紧	gǎnjǐn	Adv	at once	132
91	感冒	gǎnmào	V	to have a cold	112
92	刚才	gāngcái	N	just now	112
93	根本	gēnběn	Adv	at all	141
94	供	gōng	V	to supply	133
95	购买	gòumǎi	V	to buy	141

96	购物	gòu wù		to go shopping	141
97	古话	gǔhuà	N	old saying	153
98	骨折	gǔzhé	V	to fracture	114
99	顾客	gùkè	N	customer	131
100	挂	guà	V	to register	111
101	挂	guà	V	to hang	123
102	挂号	guà hào	V//O	to register (at a hospital, etc.)	111
103	光线	guāngxiàn	N	light	123
104	广播	guǎngbō	N	announcement	131
105	广告	guǎnggào	N	advertisement	121
106	国际	guójì	Adj/N	international	143
107	过目	guò mù	V//O	to have a look	152

H

108	海鲜	hǎixiān	N	seafood	113
109	含	hán	V	to include	151
110	好像	hǎoxiàng	Adv	as if	132
111	号	hào	N	registration	111
112	嗬	hē	Int	oh	143
113	合同	hétong	N	contract	122
114	嘿	hēi	Int	Hi	121
115	乎	hū	Pt	*an exclamatory particle that expresses doubt or indicates a rhetorical question*	153
116	护士	hùshi	N	nurse	111
117	护照	hùzhào	N	passport	131
118	划算	huásuàn	Adj	economical	133
119	化验	huàyàn	V	to test, to assay	113
120	还	huán	V	to pay back	132
121	换钱	huàn qián	V//O	to exchange money	131

122	汇款	huì kuǎn	V//O	to remit money	131
123	汇率	huìlǜ	N	exchange rate	131
124	活期	huóqī	Adj	current (deposit)	131
125	火车	huǒchē	N	train	153
126	火锅	huǒguō	N	hotpot	113
127	伙伴	huǒbàn	N	partner	143
128	或者	huòzhě	Conj	or	141
129	货	huò	N	goods	141
130	货到付款	huò dào fù kuǎn		a means of payment (especially for the online shopping), meaning that the buyer can pay after he / she receives the stuff and makes confirmation	141

J

131	几乎	jīhū	Adv	nearly, almost	141
132	机	jī	N	machine	131
133	基金	jījīn	N	fund	132
134	极	jí	Adv	extremely	152
135	急诊	jízhěn	N	emergency treatment	111
136	计划	jìhuà	V/N	to plan; plan	152
137	记	jì	V	to write down, to note	142
138	加收	jiā shōu		plus	151
139	价格	jiàgé	N	price	151
140	价目表	jiàmùbiǎo	N	price list	151
141	假条	jiàtiáo	N	note asking for leave	113
142	建议	jiànyì	V/N	to suggest; suggestion	131
143	将	jiāng	Adv	will	152
144	交	jiāo	V	to hand in	114
145	交	jiāo	V	to pay	132
146	交易	jiāoyì	N/V	transaction; to trade	143

147	接风洗尘	jiēfēng xǐchén		to give a dinner of welcome	153
148	接机	jiē jī	V//O	to meet sb. at the airport	152
149	接站	jiē zhàn	V//O	to meet sb. at the railway station	153
150	节约	jiéyuē	V	to economize, to save	143
151	尽管	jǐnguǎn	Adv	despite	153
152	紧张	jǐnzhāng	Adj	in short supply	151
153	进出口	jìn-chūkǒu		import and export	143
154	进口	jìn kǒu	V//O	to import	143
155	经常	jīngcháng	Adv	often	131
156	酒店	jiǔdiàn	N	hotel	151

K

157	卡	kǎ	N	card	131
158	开	kāi	V	to prescribe	112
159	开	kāi	V	to open	131
160	看	kàn	V	to see (a doctor)	111
161	康复	kāngfù	V	to be restored to health	114
162	考察	kǎochá	V	to investigate, to inspect	143
163	靠	kào	V	to lean against	123
164	靠近	kàojìn	V	to get near, to approach	121
165	科	kē	N	department	111
166	咳嗽	késou	V	to cough	112
167	可不是	kě bu shì		absolutely *(expressing agreement)*	143
168	客房	kèfáng	N	guest room	151
169	客厅	kètīng	N	living room	121
170	块	kuài	M	*a measure word*	123

L

171	拉肚子	lā dùzi		to suffer from diarrhoea	113

172	力	lì	N	energy, force	143
173	厉害	lìhai	Adj	terrible	111
174	利率	lìlǜ	N	interest rate	131
175	里	li	N	inside	123
176	连	lián	Prep	even	143
177	连续	liánxù	V	continuously	133
178	联系	liánxì	V	to contact	142
179	量	liáng	V	to take (one's temperature), to measure	112
180	两居室	liǎng jūshì		an apartment with two bedrooms	121
181	另外	lìngwài	Adv	in addition, besides	122
182	流	liú	V	to flow	112
183	楼道	lóudào	N	corridor	121

M

184	麻烦	máfan	Adj	troublesome	121
185	马上	mǎshàng	Adv	at once, soon	111
186	慢	màn	Adj	slow	121
187	贸易	màoyì	N	trade, business	142
188	没想到	méi xiǎngdào		unexpectedly	132
189	门诊部	ménzhěnbù	N	out-patient department	111
190	免租期	miǎnzūqī	N	rent-free period	122
191	面积	miànjī	N	area	122
192	名胜古迹	míngshèng gǔjì		place of historic interest and scenic beauty	152

N

193	拿	ná	V	to take	131
194	内科	nèikē	N	internal medicine	111
195	能干	nénggàn	Adj	capable, able	153

196	拟定	nǐdìng	V	to make, to work out	152
197	年轻	niánqīng	Adj	young	141

O

198	哦	ò	Int	*used to express realization and understanding*	132
199	欧元	ōuyuán	N	Euro	131

P

200	排队	pái duì	V//O	to line up, to queue	131
201	牌价	páijià	N	quotation	131
202	旁边	pángbiān	N	side	123
203	陪	péi	V	to accompany	114
204	陪同	péitóng	V	to accompany	152
205	喷嚏	pēntì	N	sneeze	112
206	盆	pén	N	pot, basin	123
207	片	piàn	M	piece	113
208	票	piào	N	ticket	153
209	平米	píngmǐ	N	square meter	122
210	平台	píngtái	N	platform	142
211	普通	pǔtōng	Adj	common	111

Q

212	企业	qǐyè	N	enterprise	142
213	签	qiān	V	to sign	122
214	签约	qiān yuē	V//O	to sign a contract	143
215	签字	qiān zì	V//O	to sign (one's name)	131
216	前面	qiánmian	N	front	123
217	前天	qiántiān	N	the day before yesterday	121
218	墙	qiáng	N	wall	123

219	巧	qiǎo	Adj	coincidental	132
220	请假	qǐng jià	V//O	to ask for leave	114
221	取	qǔ	V	to withdraw	131
222	取款	qǔ kuǎn		to withdraw money	131

R

223	燃气	ránqì	N	gas	132
224	人民币	rénmínbì	N	RMB	131
225	日程表	rìchéngbiǎo	N	schedule, itinerary	152
226	如果	rúguǒ	Conj	if, in case	121

S

227	嗓子	sǎngzi	N	throat	112
228	商量	shāngliang	V	to discuss	122
229	商品	shāngpǐn	N	commodity, goods	141
230	上	shàng	N	previous, last	114
231	上调	shàngtiáo	V	to raise	151
232	申请	shēnqǐng	V	to apply	141
233	生产	shēngchǎn	V	to produce, to manufacture	142
234	省	shěng	V	to save	143
235	省事	shěngshì	Adj	convenient	121
236	时差	shíchā	N	time difference	143
237	实地	shídì	Adv	on-site	143
238	适合	shìhé	V	to suit, to fit	133
239	收	shōu	V	to gain (economic benefits)	122
240	手续	shǒuxù	N	procedure	133
241	首付	shǒufù	N	down payment	133
242	受伤	shòu shāng	V//O	to be injured, to be wounded	114
243	书柜	shūguì	N	bookcase	123

244	舒服	shūfu	Adj	comfortable, well	113
245	输液	shū yè	V//O	to transfuse, to infuse	112
246	熟悉	shúxi	V	to be familiar with	141
247	刷	shuā	V	to swipe, to punch (a card)	132
248	顺便	shùnbiàn	Adv	by the way	131
249	四星级	sì xīngjí		four-star	152
250	算	suàn	V	to count as, to treat as	112
251	虽然	suīrán	Conj	though, although	123
252	随时	suíshí	Adv	at any time	122

T

253	台	tái	M	*a measure word (for home appliances)*	123
254	台历	táilì	N	desk calendar	123
255	淘	táo	V	to shop around (for sth.)	141
256	套	tào	M	*a measure word*	121
257	特价	tèjià	N	special offer	151
258	疼	téng	Adj	ache	111
259	体温	tǐwēn	N	body temperature	112
260	填	tián	V	to fill in	131
261	贴	tiē	V	to paste or stick on	121
262	停车	tíng chē	V//O	to park	122
263	停留	tíngliú	V	to stay	152
264	同	tóng	Adj	same, similar, equal	131
265	同类	tónglèi	Adj	of the same kind	152
266	头	tóu	N	head	111
267	图片	túpiàn	N	picture, photograph	141
268	推荐	tuījiàn	.V	to recommend	141

W

269	外汇	wàihuì	N	foreign exchange	131
270	外汇牌价表	wàihuì páijiàbiǎo		List of Exchange Rate Quotation	131
271	万	wàn	M	ten thousand	122
272	网上银行	wǎngshang yínháng		E-bank	141
273	网站	wǎngzhàn	N	website	141
274	网址	wǎngzhǐ	N	website address	142
275	危机	wēijī	N	crisis	143
276	卫生间	wèishēngjiān	N	washroom	121
277	为	wèi	Prep	for	152
278	文件夹	wénjiànjiā	N	file folder	123
279	卧室	wòshì	N	bedroom	121
280	物业	wùyè	N	property	122

X

281	希望	xīwàng	V	to hope	152
282	洗衣店	xǐyīdiàn	N	laundry	121
283	下面	xiàmian	N	below, under	123
284	享受	xiǎngshòu	V	to enjoy	151
285	消费	xiāofèi	V	to consume	131
286	小区	xiǎoqū	N	residential area	121
287	协议	xiéyì	N	contract	151
288	写字楼	xiězìlóu	N	office building	122
289	信息	xìnxī	N	information	142
290	信用卡	xìnyòngkǎ	N	credit card	132
291	行政间	xíngzhèngjiān	N	executive room	151
292	幸运	xìngyùn	Adj	lucky	114

293	需要	xūyào	V	to need	151
294	选	xuǎn	V	to choose	141
295	选择	xuǎnzé	V	to choose	133
296	寻找	xúnzhǎo	V	to seek, to look for	142

Y

297	呀	ya	MdPt	*a modal particle for explanation or reminding*	141
298	严重	yánzhòng	Adj	serious	113
299	阳台	yángtái	N	balcony	121
300	要求	yāoqiú	N	request	152
301	药	yào	N	medicine	112
302	要是	yàoshi	Conj	if	141
303	业务	yèwù	N	business	131
304	一定	yídìng	Adv	must, surely, certainly	121
305	一块儿	yíkuàir	Adv	together	152
306	一些	yìxiē	Q	some	123
307	一直	yìzhí	Adv	always	121
308	亦	yì	Adv	also, too	153
309	银行	yínháng	N	bank	131
310	饮水机	yǐnshuǐjī	N	water dispenser	123
311	用户	yònghù	N	client, user	142
312	优惠	yōuhuì	Adj	favorable	151
313	优先	yōuxiān	V	to have priority	151
314	由	yóu	Prep	by	152
315	邮局	yóujú	N	post office	121
316	有的	yǒude	Pr	some	121
317	有名	yǒumíng	Adj	famous, well-known	141
318	幼儿园	yòu'éryuán	N	kindergarten	121

319	诱惑力	yòuhuòlì	N	attractiveness	133
320	愉快	yúkuài	Adj	happy	153
321	遇见	yùjiàn	V	to meet	132
322	原来	yuánlái	Adv	originally	132
323	远方	yuǎnfāng	N	a distant place	153
324	越来越	yuè lái yuè		more and more	141

Z

325	杂志	zázhì	N	magazine	123
326	在线	zàixiàn	V	to be online	141
327	早日	zǎorì	Adv	early, soon	114
328	张	zhāng	V	to open	112
329	张	zhāng	M	*a measure word*	123
330	账户	zhànghù	N	account	131
331	着急	zháo jí	V//O	to get worried	121
332	折扣	zhékòu	N	discount	141
333	着	zhe	AP	*indicating the continuation of a state*	123
334	真诚	zhēnchéng	Adj	sincere	153
335	诊断证明书	zhěnduàn zhèngmíngshū		medical certificate	114
336	支付	zhīfù	V	to pay	141
337	直	zhí	Adv	directly, straight	111
338	直接	zhíjiē	Adj	direct	142
339	职员	zhíyuán	N	office worker, staff member	131
340	只是	zhǐshì	Adv	just, only	114
341	中介	zhōngjiè	N	intermediary, agent	121
342	中央	zhōngyāng	N	center	123
343	钟	zhōng	N	clock	123
344	种	zhǒng	M	a kind, a sort, a type	133

345	周围	zhōuwéi	N	surrounding	152
346	住院	zhù yuàn	V//O	to be in hospital	114
347	注意	zhù yì	V//O	to pay attention to	113
348	祝	zhù	V	to express good wishes, to wish	114
349	专家	zhuānjiā	N	expert, specialist	111
350	转	zhuǎn	V	to turn, to shift, to change	111
351	转	zhuǎn	V	to transfer, to convey	141
352	转告	zhuǎngào	V	to send word	114
353	转账	zhuǎn zhàng	V//O	to transfer accounts	131
354	转椅	zhuànyǐ	N	swivel chair	123
355	装修	zhuāngxiū	V	to decorate, to renovate	122
356	撞	zhuàng	V	to bump	114
357	桌子	zhuōzi	N	desk, table	123
358	资料	zīliào	N	material	123
359	自	zì	Prep	from, since	153
360	自动	zìdòng	Adj	automatic	131
361	自动取款机	zìdòng qǔkuǎnjī		ATM	131
362	自己	zìjǐ	Pr	oneself	122
363	总部	zǒngbù	N	headquarters	142
364	总机	zǒngjī	N	telephone exchange	151
365	租	zū	V	to rent	121
366	租售部	zūshòubù	N	rental and sales department	122
367	组	zǔ	M	*a measure word*	123
368	嘴	zuǐ	N	mouth	112
369	最好	zuìhǎo	Adv	had better	121
370	最后	zuìhòu	N	end, at last	133
371	左边	zuǒbian	N	left, left side	123
372	左手	zuǒshǒu	N	left hand	114

167

专有名词
Proper Nouns

A				
1	阿里巴巴	Ālǐbābā	the name of a commercial website	142
D				
2	当当网	Dāngdāng Wǎng	dangdang.com, an online shopping website	141
G				
3	广交会	Guǎngjiāohuì	Canton Fair *(another name of China Import and Export Fair)*	143
4	广州	Guǎngzhōu	name of a Chinese city	143
L				
5	蓝天大厦	Lántiān Dàshà	the Blue Sky Tower	122
M				
6	麦克	Màikè	Mike	152
N				
7	鸟巢	Niǎocháo	Bird's Nest (Beijing National Stadium / Olympic Stadium)	152
Q				
8	钱	Qián	a Chinese surname	122
S				
9	水立方	Shuǐlìfāng	Water Cube (The National Aquatics Center)	152

10	四海大酒店	Sìhǎi Dà Jiǔdiàn	Sihai Hotel	151
T				
11	淘宝网	Táobǎo Wǎng	taobao.com, an online shopping website	141
Z				
12	支付宝	Zhīfùbǎo	alipay.com, an online payment platform	141
13	中国进出口商品交易会	Zhōngguó Jìn-chūkǒu Shāngpǐn Jiāoyìhuì	China Import and Export Fair	143
14	卓越网	Zhuóyuè Wǎng	amazon.cn, an online shopping website	141

汉语1000常用字
1000 Frequently Used Chinese Characters

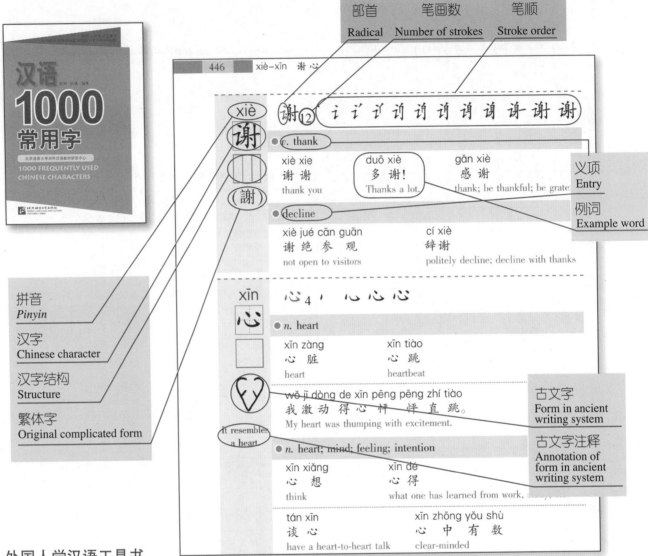

部首	笔画数	笔顺
Radical	Number of strokes	Stroke order

446   xiè–xīn   谢 心

xiè 谢⑫ 讠 讠 讠 诮 诮 诮 诮 诮 谢 谢

谢 / 谢

- *v.* thank

xiè xie — 谢谢 — thank you
duō xiè — 多谢! — Thanks a lot.
gǎn xiè — 感谢 — thank; be thankful; be grate...

- decline

xiè jué cān guān — 谢绝参观 — not open to visitors
cí xiè — 辞谢 — politely decline; decline with thanks

xīn 心₄ 丶 心 心 心

心

- *n.* heart

xīn zàng — 心脏 — heart
xīn tiào — 心跳 — heartbeat

It resembles a heart

wǒ jī dòng de xīn pēng pēng zhí tiào — 我激动得心怦 怦直跳。— My heart was thumping with excitement.

- *n.* heart; mind; feeling; intention

xīn xiǎng — 心想 — think
xīn dé — 心得 — what one has learned from work,...

tán xīn — 谈心 — have a heart-to-heart talk
xīn zhōng yǒu shù — 心中有数 — clear-minded

义项 Entry
例词 Example word
古文字 Form in ancient writing system
古文字注释 Annotation of form in ancient writing system

拼音 Pinyin
汉字 Chinese character
汉字结构 Structure
繁体字 Original complicated form

外国人学汉语工具书
CHINESE REFERENCE SERIES FOR FOREIGNERS

- 收录最常用汉字1000个。

  With 1000 most frequently used Chinese characters

- 例词、例句简单实用，贴近生活。

  With example words and sentences that are simple, practical and close to life

- 提供音序、笔画、部首多种检字法，便于检索。

  With multiple indexing systems to help locate the characters, including phonetic indexing, stroke indexing and radical indexing

ISBN 978-7-5619-2703-8

定价：55.00元

实用汉语分级阅读丛书
Step-by-Step Chinese Reading for Practical Purposes

崔永华 总主编

- **开本**：小16开
- **注释文种**：英文/韩文/日文

本套丛书根据《汉语水平词汇与汉字等级大纲》分为甲、乙、丙、丁四个等级，可以由学生根据自己的汉语水平选择合适的分册。书中的文章多选自报纸和杂志，内容涉及中国的现状和中国人生活的方方面面。本套丛书可以帮助学生更好地认读汉字、识记生词，提高汉语水平，增加对中国的了解。

甲级读本 Level 1

书　名		相关话题
我在中国的那些日子	When I was in China	留学生活
我在中国的那些日子2	When I was in China 2	留学生活

乙级读本 Level 2

书　名		相关话题
从"一窍不通"到"胸有成竹"	From a Layman to a Professional	成语故事
从"坐井观天"到"鹏程万里"	From the Bottom to the Top	成语故事
中国人有趣的实话实说	Chinese People Like to Speak the Truth	中国人
中国人喜欢跳舞	Chinese People Like to Dance	中国事
中国的"负翁"越来越多	There Are More and More Indebted Persons in China	中国经济
中国教育跟西方不一样	China's Education is Different from that of Western Countries	中国教育
我当上了中国女婿	I Married a Chinese Girl	中国情感
砍价是一种享受	Bargaining Is a Kind of Enjoyment	生活感悟
我是世界上最幽默的人	I'm the Most Humorous Person in the World	语言·文化

丙级读本 Level 3

书　名		相关话题
用明天的钱，实现今天的梦	Use Tomorrow's Money to Fulfil Today's Dream	中国经济·生活

Embark on your Chinese learning from the website of
Beijing Language and Culture University Press

北京语言大学出版社网站：**www.blcup.com**

从这里开始······

International online orders
TEL: +86-10-82303668
+86-10-82303080
Email: service@blcup.net

这里是对外汉语精品教材的展示平台

汇集2000余种对外汉语教材，检索便捷，
每本教材有目录、简介、样课等详尽信息。

It showcases BLCUP's superb textbooks of TCFL (Teaching Chinese as a Foreign Language)

It has a collection of more than 2,000 titles of BLCUP's TCFL textbooks, which are easy to be searched, with details such as table of contents, brief introduction and sample lessons for each textbook.

这里是覆盖全球的电子商务平台

在任何地点，均可通过VISA/MASTER卡在线购买。

It provides an e-commerce platform which covers the whole world.

Online purchase with VISA/MASTER Card can be made in every part of the world.

这里是数字出版的体验平台

只需在线支付，即刻就可获取质高价优的全新电子图书。

It provides digital publication service.

A top-grade and reasonably-priced brand new e-book can be obtained as soon as you pay for it online.

这里是对外汉语教学／学习资源的服务平台

提供测试题、知识讲解、阅读短文、教案、课件、教学示范、教材配套资料等各类文字、音视频资源。

It provides a service platform for Chinese language learning for foreigners.

All kinds of written and audio-visual teaching resources are available, including tests, explanations on language points, reading passages, teaching plans, courseware, teaching demo and other supplementary teaching materials etc.

这里是沟通交流的互动平台

汉语教学与学习论坛，使每个参与者都能共享海量信息与资源。

It provides a platform for communication.

This platform for Chinese teaching and learning makes it possible for every participant to share our abundant data and resources.